In-Person

A Journey Through the Unstoppable Evolution of Events

**Mapping the Power
of Collective Human Gatherings
to Co-Create the Future**

By Enrico Gallorini

Dedication

A special thank you to Elisa, Emma and Elena
for their love, support, and patience
throughout this long journey.

And a heartfelt thank you to you,
the reader I wish you smiles and positive
thoughts throughout this adventure...

Events are, by their nature, FANTASTIC!

Epigraph

An event is like a soap bubble
it captivates and enchants in the moment but vanishes swiftly,
leaving behind an experience that words can never fully capture.

Events are the purest form of ephemeral art
beautiful and unique
destined to disappear almost immediately
yet their legacy lasts forever.

Table of Contents

PART 2: THE ART & SCIENCE OF EVENT ORGANIZING

PART 3: THE FUTURE OF EVENTS

Foreword:
The Timeless Power of Events

by Geoff Dickinson

What do the grand spectacles of ancient Rome, the intellectual salons of the Renaissance, and the vibrant large events of today have in common? How have events reflected and shaped our societies, and how have our events and gatherings evolved? Will they evolve as our civilization changes? And perhaps most importantly: What can exploring these questions teach us about the significance of events and their power to shape our world to create a better future?

These are just some of the questions that will be explored in the pages ahead.

As someone deeply immersed in the events industry, it is both an honor and a pleasure to introduce this remarkable work by Enrico Gallorini. My journey in this field has allowed me to witness firsthand the transformative power of gatherings and the profound impact they have on individuals and communities.

I have had the pleasure of knowing Enrico Gallorini for years, both as a colleague and a friend. His passion for events and relentless pursuit of excellence in this field are truly inspiring. Enrico's unique ability to blend historical insight with practical knowledge makes him the perfect guide for this exploration to better understand the present of our industry and the possible future of human gatherings.

This book explores the fascinating evolution of events, from the earliest communal rituals to the grand spectacles of business and government events and the power they wield in the modern era. It reveals how events have shaped and been shaped by society, acting as catalysts for human progress and cultural exchange. By delving into the rich history of events, we uncover the enduring significance of these gatherings and their impact on human culture and evolution in the future

Throughout the millennia of human history, events and gatherings have been the beating heart of our collective experience, each one a reflection of its time, its people, and their creativity and dreams. From the dawn of human civilization, events have played a pivotal role in shaping our collective identity and fostering societal progress. In the early days, gatherings around the fire were not just about survival; they were moments of storytelling, teaching, and co-creation. These gatherings laid the foundation for more complex social structures and cultural practices.

Events and gatherings are not just moments of convergence; they are profound catalysts that shape our identities, cultures, and societies. When we come together, whether around a fire, in grand stadiums, or through business-oriented collective experiences, we share knowledge, information, and technologies that mold our collective consciousness. These shared moments foster a sense of community, ignite innovation, and inspire change, imprinting upon us the values and narratives that define our times.

Enrico's work is a testament to his deep understanding and appreciation of the art and science of event organizing. But not just that, they reflect his deep love of ideas, art, culture, friendship and humanity itself. His insights into the historical, cultural, and practical aspects of events provide a comprehensive and enlightening perspective that will benefit both professionals and enthusiasts alike. This book is a must-read for anyone looking to understand the importance of events and the profound impact they have on human history and their potential to shape the future.

The book is neatly divided into three parts that represent the three main dimensions of the author's inquiry: the past, the present, and the future.

Part 1 is a historical journey that traces the origins and evolution of human gatherings and events from their origin.

In **Part 2**, moving to the present, Enrico shares his unique life path, revealing how bringing people together seems to have been fated for him. This part also explores the art and science of event organizing today and what goes into creating and hosting impactful events.

Finally, **Part 3** looks into the cutting edge of the event industry, including a speculative vision into the future of events and what the next innovations and evolutions will be.

Enrico makes the case that the role and importance of the Event Industry will be even more important in the future, when AI and new technology will make it difficult to differentiate between what is true and what is false. Events cannot be faked, and therefore the live in-person experience will become increasingly valuable.

I am excited for you to join Enrico Gallorini on this journey through time and space—as he uncovers the rich history of human gatherings and explores the profound impact they have had on our world. Whether you are an event organizer, a history enthusiast, or simply curious about the stories and meanings behind our everyday gatherings and celebrations, there is something here for you. This book will take you from the past to the present and into the future, exploring the role of events in human history, their impact on cultural and societal evolution, and the innovations shaping the events of tomorrow.

Through historical analysis, personal anecdotes, industry insights, and future speculations, Enrico Gallorini uncovers the timeless power of events and their enduring significance in our lives. You'll also gain insights and foundational principles for how to create, organize, and host powerful, joyful, and transformative events in your own life. You couldn't be in better hands as a guide on the journey behind the gatherings that have shaped our world.

Geoff Dickinson

INTRODUCTION

Why this book?

In every era, events and gatherings have been the heartbeat and lifeblood of human culture, reflecting our shared values, aspirations, and dreams. As we journey through time, these archetypal forms of human connection continue to evolve, each one a testament to the enduring power of coming together and the creativity and innovation that inevitably occurs.

The initial inspiration for this book was to contemplate the future of the event industry. However, when we attempt to predict the future, we encounter many uncertainties because, of course, it remains ultimately unknown. However, in my thinking I try to follow the leading futurists who often echo the mantra: "The further back you can look, the further forward you are likely to see."

We are now entering a historical period characterized by rapid change, making it crucial to understand the mechanisms of past transformations to better comprehend the present and anticipate the future. The massive digital transformation, driven now primarily by the AI revolution that is just beginning, is one of humanity's most pivotal evolutions, reminiscent of previous times when humans and technology evolved together. This evolution owes much to the role of meetings, events, and exhibitions, as we will explore in various chapters of this book.

The future is full of possibilities where technology and imagination blend seamlessly. In a world transformed by AI, augmented reality, and quantum computing, events take on a new dimension. Imagine participants from everywhere gathering in a holographic space station orbiting earth AI concierges guide them through personalized experiences tailored to individual interests and needs. Immersive simulations allow attendees to step into different worlds, from ancient civilizations to alien landscapes. These futuristic events are the marriage of technology and human creativity, pushing the boundaries of what gatherings can be and uniting people in ways previously unimaginable. Yet underlying it all, no matter how much our technology advances, lies the centrality of eternal face-to-face human interaction, and the power of the "in-person" experience.

In my own life, I have found myself repeatedly drawn to the act of bringing people together. Whether working behind the scenes or engaging directly with participants, I have witnessed the unique alchemy that happens when people gather to create a shared experience. This fascination has fueled my passion for exploring the magic that occurs in these moments of connection and collaboration.

In this book, I want to share that excitement with you. It is my hope that we all come to realize the profound significance and power of events and gatherings in our lives—culturally, technologically, spiritually, and beyond.

This book is a culmination of years of exploration and research in the field, and I am thrilled to start this journey with you, and share the stories and insights uncovered along the way. To grasp the full picture, this book delves into the history of the event industry from its inception. While thinking about exactly when events started, each time I thought I had reached the beginning, I discovered that there was even more before that point. As you will see, this journey took me quite far back, revealing the deep roots and enduring significance of human gatherings.

We will journey back to the earliest beginnings of human culture and project forward to the near and distant future. We will be guided by the ubiquitous centrality of human gatherings and events as catalysts for our evolution. These moments of connection are the building blocks of our collective human experience, from ancient rituals to modern-day conferences. If storytelling is our "secret power" and the most important differentiation of Homo sapiens from any other animals, the events were, are and will be the tool to leverage our stories.

This book is an exploration of how our collective experiences, shared through events and gatherings, have propelled human progress. Join me as we uncover the timeless essence of these moments and their impact on our culture, technology, and civilization. Together, we will see how understanding our past can illuminate the path to our future.

So now, this introduction has arrived at its end... It is time to start our journey! Let us begin at the beginning, where the first sparks of socialization ignited the fire of human culture and set us on a path of endless possibilities...

Enrico Gallorini

Gatherings Through the Ages

In the dim glow of the firelight, shadows dance on the walls of the cave. The earliest humans huddle close, the warmth of the flames a comfort against the night's chill. Here, under the vast expanse of starlit skies, they share news of the hunt, weave tales of ancestors, and sing songs that echo with the rhythms of the earth. The fire is their hearth, their gathering point, where stories bind them together in a shared legacy of survival and wonder.

At dawn, the first light of the sun kisses the ziggurat's towering facade, casting long shadows across the city of Ur. Clad in ceremonial robes, a procession of priests and priestesses ascends the sacred steps, their chants rising with the morning mist. In the heart of ancient Sumeria, the community gathers to honor the gods, offering grain, wine, and incense. The air is thick with the scent of burning offerings, and as prayers are lifted to the heavens, the people are united in their devotion, seeking favor and harmony from the divine.

The sun blazes high over the plains of Olympia, casting a golden glow over the assembled crowd. Athletes from distant city-states, their bodies honed to perfection, prepare to compete in the first ancient Greek Olympic Games. Cheers erupt as runners sprint down the dusty track, their feet pounding as if as an echo of the very heartbeat of Greece itself. These games are more than mere competition they are a celebration of human excellence and unity under the watchful eyes of the gods.

In the grandeur of the Colosseum, the roar of the crowd rises as if being expressed by a single living creature. The vast architectural marvel that is the amphitheater trembles with anticipation. Gladiators, clad in gleaming armor, stand ready to fight for glory and survival. Exotic beasts from the far corners of the empire are unleashed, and the spectacle of combat and bravery unfolds. The emperor's thumb dictates life or death, and the Roman populace, united in their bloodlust and excitement, are witnesses to the drama that epitomizes the might and spectacle of Rome.

The village square is transformed into a vibrant m lange of colors and sounds. Merchants from far and wide set up stalls brimming with goods spices from the East, fine textiles, and handcrafted wares. Jugglers, minstrels, and jesters entertain the bustling crowds, while knights in shining armor joust for honor and the favor of fair maidens. The air is filled with laughter, music, and the mingling aromas of roasting meats and sweet pastries. Here, in the heart of the Medieval Faire, the community gathers to fulfill many of medieval society's most important functions in one single event.

In a richly adorned chamber, the air is thick with the scent of candle wax and parchment, and the air is alive with the hum of conversation. Scholars, artists, and philosophers gather to debate and share ideas that challenge the very fabric of society. The host, a patron of the arts, orchestrates these gatherings with grace, providing a space where minds can meet and ignite the sparks of innovation. Discussions on art, science, politics, and philosophy weave together in the Renaissance intellectual salon, and the effects of these small gatherings lead to world-changing revolutions and paradigm shifts.

The Crystal Palace stands as a shimmering beacon of progress in the heart of London. Inside, the Great Exhibition of 1851 unfolds, a showcase of human ingenuity and industrial achievement. Nations from around the world present their finest innovations steam engines, intricate machinery, and exotic goods. The air is thick with excitement and the promise of a new era. Visitors marvel at the wonders on display, their imaginations ignited by the possibilities of the future. The very first worldwide international expo is attended by over 6 million visitors and the stage is now set for future international expositions.

In the summer of 1969, as the sun set over the rolling hills of Bethel, New York, a sea of people have gathered in the middle of a farmer's field The air is thick with the mingling scents of grass, earth, and marijuana, On the stage, Indian sitar master Ravi Shankar plays a deeply meditative yet joyful raga while Jimi Hendrix and other western rock and pop stars watch from the audience. Draped in colorful, flowing garments, young men and women sway in unison, and their movements seem to shake off the restrictions of the past and summon forth a collective consciousness desire for peace, love, and a new way of being. Woodstock was more than a concert it was a cultural watershed, a moment when the counterculture's ideals crystallized, leaving an indelible mark on the fabric of society.

Under the neon-tinged skyline of Dubai and within the sprawling convention halls of the DWTC, the whole city has come alive with a hum of anticipation for the biggest event in the world Gitex Global 2024. Throngs of tech enthusiasts, industry professionals, and thought leaders converge from all over the world within these halls and around the city while visions of tomorrow are unveiled AI-driven marvels, immersive virtual realities, and sustainable technologies poised to reshape our world. As presentations unfold and deals are struck, a collective sense of awe and possibility permeates the air. Here, in this crucible of creativity, the world's brightest minds gather, united in their devotion to advancing humanity's journey into the digital age, forging connections, and inspiring the next wave of global transformation.

In the year 2075, as the sun's first rays glint off the sleek, towering spires of Tokyo, a global expo unfolds. Attendees glide along pathways lined with bioluminescent flora while a symphony of different languages drifts out from holographic displays dancing overhead, Within this massive event, innovations that blur the lines between the physical and digital realms are unveiled quantum computing marvels, interstellar travel breakthroughs, and technologies that harmonize with nature to heal the planet.

Within each pavilion, novel solutions to the world's most pressing challenges are presented. The centerpiece of the exhibition is the in-process project of terraforming and colonizing Mars, where live feeds from the red planet allow attendees to witness the transformation in real time. As global leaders, scientists, artists, and dreamers gather, they inspire and challenge each other to greater heights and revel in the excitement of collaboration and co-creation.

For those attending in person, the experience is full and immersive and tactile, with interactive exhibits and sensory displays that engage all senses. Simultaneously, Billions around the world and even those stationed in craft and stations near Earth orbit participate through advanced virtual reality interfaces, experiencing the event as if they were physically present.

In the centuries to come, this event stands out as a major milestone on Humanity's journey to a harmonious collective civilization that makes the quantum leap to the stars.

THE EVOLUTION OF HUMAN EVENTS

PART

1

The Dawn of Socialization: Our Earliest Ancestors

In the twilight of a cool summer evening, the soft glow of a campfire flickers against the rugged stone walls of a hidden valley. The air is filled with the soothing crackle of burning wood and the hum of excited conversations. Kiro, a young man known for his quick mind and nimble fingers, sits among his tribe. Tonight is special two tribes have come together, sharing a rare moment of peace and exchange. The leaders of each tribe have met and decided to trade rather than fight.

As the moon climbs higher, shadows emerge figures carrying bundles and strange objects. Among the newcomers is Tarek, an elder known for his wisdom. He unwraps a bundle, revealing finely crafted stones and wooden handles. With precise movements, Tarek demonstrates how to bind stones to handles using tree sap and ash. Eager to learn, Kiro approaches Tarek, who shows him each step in the crafting process.

Kiro's eyes widen as he realizes the potential of this new tool a spearhead that is not only sharper but also more durable than anything his tribe has ever seen. Inspired, Kiro's mind races with possibilities. He sees how this tool could change their hunting techniques, making them more efficient and allowing them to secure food with greater ease.

In exchange, members of Kiro's tribe share unique resources and technologies passed down by their ancestors. Women from the tribe demonstrate a unique way of cooking a plant to extract a medicine substance for healing purposes, while a wise elder shares knowledge on navigating by the stars. These exchanges, filled with curiosity and respect, weave the two tribes closer together. Whereas before there had been incidents of conflict and violence, now there is mutual respect and excitement at learning from one another.

Through this gathering or event, they were able overcome their conflict and co-create a better future. By the end of the night, Kiro crafts his first spearhead, and the next day, his tribe has a very successful hunt, which they gladly share with their new allies.

From the earliest days of humanity, gatherings such as this have been a cornerstone of our social fabric. The central fire, with its light and warmth, served as the nexus point for these gatherings, providing an attractive and inviting space for interaction and collaboration. Around this fire, people shared meals, told stories, sang songs, and exchanged ideas.

These gatherings often coincided with astronomically significant days, such as solstices and equinoxes, or to celebrate events like a successful hunt or the crowning of a new chief.

The fire's circle was more than just a place to keep warm; it was the first event space that fostered connection and creativity. As the flames flickered, individuals gazed up at the stars, pondering their mysteries and weaving tales of what they might mean. The myths and legends told about the stars, the land, and the people were the spiritual and religious framework that held up the entire society and gave a collective and individual sense of meaning and purpose.

In this sacred circle of light, each group member contributed to the collective narrative. The elder would speak of the spirits of the land, the animals, and the ancestors who watched over them. These stories were the foundation of the community's beliefs and values, more than mere entertainment—they were essential teachings passed down through generations.

As the night deepened, simple rituals took place, binding the group together. A portion of the meal might be offered to the fire as a gesture of gratitude to the spirits, or a dance might be performed to mimic the hunt, celebrating survival and abundance. These rituals, though simple, carried profound significance, creating a sense of order and meaning that were essential for further steps on the ladder of evolution.

This scene, repeated countless times over millennia, is the foundation upon which human civilization is built. These gatherings were not just about survival; they were about creating a sense of community and identity, about connecting with each other and with something greater than themselves. This stage in our evolution marked the dawn of socialization, where the roots of our culture, religion, art, and science began to take hold.

As we explore the history and evolution of human events and gatherings in this book, everything has its roots in these primal scenes. The essence of these early gatherings is still with us today, in every festival, fair, exhibition, concert, large event, conference, and family reunion. No matter how sophisticated our events become, the fundamental need to connect, share, and belong remains unchanged. And I think you will agree that the essential way that we gather and hold events has not really changed in essence, but only in external form.

Socialization and the Cognitive Revolution

We start our exploration of the evolution of events around 70,000 years ago with the Cognitive Revolution. During this time, Homo sapiens developed advanced cognitive abilities, allowing for complex language, abstract thinking, and intricate social structures.

Before this revolution, early humans lived in small, isolated groups, communicating through basic sounds and gestures. Gatherings and events would've been minimal in power, as early humans did not have the linguistic and cognitive abilities to engage in higher-order creative, scientific, or technological activities.

One of the most significant advancements was the development of complex language. This enabled early humans to convey abstract concepts, future plans, and shared beliefs, facilitating the formation of larger, cohesive groups. Language allowed for the detailed sharing of knowledge about the environment, survival strategies, and cultural practices, creating a sense of identity and unity within communities.

The evolutionary advantages of socialization were profound. By forming social bonds, early humans could protect each other, improve hunting strategies, and share resources more effectively. Empathy and cooperation became essential for survival, fostering mutual support and community stability. These social bonds were reinforced through communal activities and rituals, maintaining group cohesion.

Around the fireside, early humans shared experiences, discussed hunting strategies, and taught younger members about their world. These interactions laid the groundwork for social institutions such as clans and tribes. Rituals emerged as a key component of social life, expressing shared values and beliefs and establishing social hierarchies. As socialization grew more complex, early humans developed culture, including art, music, and symbolic expression. All this was made possible by the rapid advances in cognitive capacity all those years ago, and all of those elements were possible because of the social sharing during events.

The author and historian Yuval Noah Harari argues that the superpower of Homo Sapiens is storytelling because it allows humans to create and share complex social constructs, foster large-scale cooperation, and build and maintain societies. This ability to invent and believe in shared myths and narratives differentiates humans from other species and has enabled our evolutionary success. Having very few means of physical defense, Homo sapiens have had to exploit this storytelling ability to survive and thrive. Furthermore, the importance of storytelling is rooted in events, which are the places, times, and spaces where storytelling occurs. Thus, events are the foundation of evolution, providing the context and medium through which the superpower of storytelling operates and drives human progress.

The Birth of Rituals & Myths

Imagine standing in the dim light of the vast Lascaux Cave in France as you view the 17,000-year-old paintings of hunting scenes and animals on the walls.The images seem to come alive in the flickering and dancing light of torches and cease to be two-dimensional primitive drawings, but rather become a living film conveying something profound. You realize that these works of art may have served the same purpose as an epic Star Wars movie does today.

Think of the people in our dim past who painted these scenes. What stories were they telling? What rituals do these pictures depict, and how were they used to help them make sense of their world?

From the very beginning, humans have used myths and rituals to explain the mysteries of life and to connect with each other. These foundational elements of culture are deeply intertwined, shaping our understanding of the world and our place within it.

Rituals, symbolic actions performed in a prescribed order with a specific purpose and meaning, are the cornerstone of human culture. Rituals can be religious or secular and typically involve repetition, community participation, and the use of symbols. The repetition of the ritual drives home the message through the act of enacting it repeatedly. Rituals create order, convey cultural values, and reinforce social bonds. For early humans, rituals were crucial for establishing shared identity, reinforcing social bonds, and providing structure to their communities. They offered frameworks for comprehending natural phenomena, life cycles, and social hierarchies, fostering unity and cooperation.

Archaeological evidence, such as the Shanidar Cave in Iraq, reveals that some Neanderthals buried their dead with flowers. This seemingly simple act indicates symbolic, ritualistic behavior and a belief in an afterlife, honoring the deceased and reinforcing social bonds among the living. Similarly, the Blombos Cave in South Africa, with its 73,000-year-old cross-hatched drawing and ochre carvings, suggests early humans engaged in symbolic behavior and personal adornment, key components of ritualistic practices. These symbols conveyed social status and cultural beliefs, highlighting the value placed on community and tradition.

In today's world, rituals are fundamental to the event industry. Everyone knows that the Olympics occur every four years, and the FIFA World Cup, another highly popular event, also takes place every four years. The Super Bowl is always held on the first Sunday of February. Many major exhibitions across various industries adhere to a consistent schedule, whether annually or biennially, following the seasonal patterns of each niche. This ritualistic timing is one of the unique selling propositions of these important events.

Rituals go hand-in-hand and play a vital role in myth-making and storytelling. Gatherings for rituals facilitated sharing stories and myths, providing frameworks for understanding the world. These narratives, passed down through generations, became integral to cultural heritage. Early human gatherings were ripe with storytelling, where individuals shared tales explaining natural phenomena, historical events, and moral lessons. These stories were more than entertainment; they were educational tools imparting wisdom and survival strategies. Myths often involve gods, heroes, and ancestors, providing a sense of continuity and connection to the past and fostering a shared identity and a sense of belonging among group members.

The power of myths and stories lies in their ability to connect individuals to a larger narrative, creating a sense of purpose and meaning. As we continue to gather to enact ritualistic activity and share stories today, we maintain this ancient tradition of communal learning and cultural transmission.

Understanding the birth of rituals and the power of myths and stories reveals the fundamental nature of human gatherings—moments of connection, meaning, and shared humanity. These early rituals and stories have laid the foundation for the rich well of human culture, highlighting the enduring power of creativity and the deep need for connection that defines us. As we explore the evolution of human events and gatherings, it becomes clear that while rituals and stories have grown complex, their essence remains unchanged: they are about creating meaning, sharing knowledge, and reinforcing social bonds.

Whether it is a political rally, an exhibition, or a festival like Burning Man, we still create ritual events that reflect our innate need for connection and the creation of shared meaning. At these events, rituals are enacted and myths are shared.These myths and rituals contain the magical power to change human consciousness and the course of our civilization and world.

Human Connection:
The Importance of Gathering

I invite you to return in your imagination to our ancient ancestors huddled around a campfire, their faces flickering in the warm glow, sharing tales of the hunt and weaving myths that explained the stars above. From these earliest rituals, what has been at the heart of our existence is human connection. These gatherings, whether in the glow of a fire or the grandeur of a temple, have always been about more than survival. They have been about creating a shared sense of meaning and community. They are about having fun and sharing the experience of life with our friends, family, and strangers who could become friends.

Humans are inherently social creatures, driven by a deep-seated need to connect. Why do we gather? Because the essence of human connection lies in shared experiences and mutual understanding. From intimate family dinners to sprawling public events, when people gather, they share thoughts, ideas, and emotions, creating a synergy that often leads to innovation and progress.

The unique ability of Homo sapiens to cooperate in large numbers, even with strangers, sets us apart from other animals, which typically need to know each other or be part of the same family or tribe to work together. This limitation significantly restricts the scalability of cooperation in other species. Our ability to collaborate on a large scale has been crucial for human evolution, and it is fundamentally based on the trust humans create.

This trust is established through moments where people come together and build connections, even if they do not know each other. These moments occur during events and gatherings, highlighting the importance of such occasions in fostering large-scale cooperation. Thus, events are not merely social gatherings; they are essential for developing the trust and cooperation that drive human progress.

In the realm of business events, such as exhibitions and trade fairs, we see the highest expression of "co-opetition"—a blend of cooperation and competition. Outside these events, companies may compete fiercely, but within the context of the event, they cooperate for the good of the industry. This unique dynamic showcases how events can unite competitors in a way that benefits everyone involved, driving innovation and progress.

Gatherings serve multiple purposes: they reinforce social bonds, facilitate the exchange of knowledge, and provide a sense of belonging. From the earliest communal rituals to modern conferences and festivals, these events create spaces where individuals connect personally and collectively. This connection transcends physical proximity; it's about the emotional and intellectual exchanges that occur when people come together.

Think about it: When humans gather, they do more than just coexist. They collaborate, inspire, and support each other. This collective effort leads to the development of culture, technology, and societal norms. The archetypal significance of gatherings lies in their ability to transform individual experiences into a shared narrative, shaping our understanding of the world and our place in it.

Consider Göbekli Tepe in Turkey, the world's oldest known temple complex, dating back to around 9600 BC. Massive stone pillars arranged in circles suggest that early humans gathered for ritual purposes even before agriculture. This site indicates that the drive to gather and perform rituals was a fundamental aspect of early human society, possibly even motivating the development of settled communities.

At the core of every event, whether a simple family meal or a grand international expo, is the human desire for connection. These gatherings are moments of storytelling, learning, and celebration. They allow us to share our achievements, mourn our losses, and envision our future together. But most of all, these gatherings create the all-important trust that is at the base of social evolution, and that is one of the cornerstones of why events are so important - this trust allows us to cooperate on a large scale.

In our complex, technologically advanced world, it's essential to remember the simple, primitive nature of gatherings that we carry within us. The basic elements of events—connection, storytelling, and shared experiences—remain unchanged. These elements are deeply embedded in our DNA, a legacy from our earliest ancestors that continues to shape our interactions and experiences. The essence of human connection is timeless, reflecting the enduring power of coming together to create, share, and grow as a community.

The timeless nature of gatherings is a testament to the enduring power of human connection. As we evolve and innovate, we must hold on to these fundamental aspects of our humanity. Whether through virtual platforms or in-person events, the essence of coming together remains a vital part of our lives. This enduring legacy of connection and community will continue to shape our future, just as it has shaped our past.

Ritualistic Gathering
and Civilizational Evolution

Human history is a vibrant tapestry woven from countless threads of collective effort, shared knowledge, and communal experiences. At the very heart of this intricate tapestry are events and ritualistic gatherings. These gatherings have sparked creativity, driven innovation, and transmitted ideas across generations. We must remember that our progress is not the result of isolated geniuses but a continuous chain of shared human experiences.

What sets Homo sapiens apart from other species? It's our unique proclivity to gather. While many creatures exhibit social tendencies, the depth and complexity of human social structures are unparalleled. Our drive to assemble transcends basic survival instincts, reflecting a profound yearning for emotional and intellectual connection. This drive for social interconnectedness has catalyzed cultural innovation and given rise to civilizations. It underscores the intrinsic value we place on community and belonging, elements as crucial to our species' past as they are to our future.

When people come together for events, something magical happens. Ideas are exchanged, perspectives blended, and new thoughts inspired. The synergy that occurs when people gather is a powerful force. It allows for the cross-pollination of ideas and the combination of skills and knowledge that no single individual could achieve alone. The evolution of civilization is a testament to the power of these collective efforts.

In the communal firelight of our earliest ancestors, stories were told, experiences were shared, rituals were acted out, and knowledge was passed down. These gatherings were not just about survival; they were incubators of innovation. The first tools, the initial sparks of art, and the rudimentary understanding of science were all born from these communal interactions.

We stand on the shoulders of giants, benefiting from the accumulated wisdom and achievements of countless individuals who came together to share their insights and push the boundaries of what is possible. Every invention, every piece of art, every scientific breakthrough is part of a continuum that extends back to those earliest gatherings around the campfire. These communal experiences have always been the engine of human progress, propelling us forward and building the foundation upon which modern civilization stands.

The ritualistic gatherings of our ancestors laid the groundwork for the advanced societies we live in today. By coming together to celebrate, learn, and innovate, we continue to honor that ancient tradition and drive forward the evolution of our species. These gatherings are more than just events; they are the bedrock of human achievement - the spaces where our collective potential is realized and our future is shaped.

As we conclude this chapter, envision the vast sky of human history—each star a story, each constellation a gathering that guided our way. Our journey from hunter-gatherers to settled societies is just beginning. In the next chapter, we will explore how the rise of rituals transformed these early communities into the complex, dynamic civilizations that laid the groundwork for our world today. Our adventure through the annals of human event-making is just getting started.

CHAPTER 02

From Hunter Gatherers to Settled Societies: The Rise of Rituals

The sun is rising on a small, sun-drenched valley nestled between rolling hills, where a river's gentle flow sustains a burgeoning community. The air is filled with the earthy scent of freshly tilled soil and the sounds of laughter and conversation as families work side by side in the fields. Simple, thatched huts dot the landscape, smoke curling from their hearths as evening meals are prepared. Children chase each other around patches of golden wheat while elders sit in circles, weaving baskets and sharing stories.

This is one of the earliest settlements where nomadic hunters and gatherers have chosen to put down roots. The shift from a life of wandering to one of stability came with the discovery that seeds scattered in the ground could yield a bountiful harvest. No longer needing to follow the herds or search endlessly for food, these early agriculturalists found a new rhythm in the seasons. They celebrated the planting and harvest with communal feasts, giving thanks to the earth for its abundance. This newfound ability to produce and store food brought security and allowed their culture to flourish, marking the dawn of settled human civilization.

As these early settlers embraced the stability of agricultural life, their religious rituals and communal gatherings transformed dramatically. With the sun and seasons now dictating their livelihoods, they began to observe festivals aligned with the agricultural calendar—spring planting, midsummer growth, and autumn harvest.

These festivals became grand events, filled with music, dance, and feasting, binding the community together in shared celebration and reverence. Their rituals evolved from simple prayers for successful hunts to elaborate ceremonies invoking the blessings of nature's cycles. The need to trade surplus goods fostered interactions with neighboring settlements, leading to larger gatherings where ideas, customs, and technologies were exchanged. These inter-community events were the precursors to markets and fairs, planting the seeds for the complex web of social and economic interactions that would define human civilizations for millennia. Through these gatherings, the rhythm of communal life was punctuated with moments of profound connection, underscoring the enduring importance of events in shaping our social fabric.

The Transition from Nomadic to Settled Life

We human beings were hunter-gatherers for the vast majority of our history. Homo sapiens emerged around 300,000 years ago, and the shift to agricultural societies began only around 12,000 years ago. This means that human beings lived as hunter-gatherers for about 288,000 years, which constitutes roughly 95-96% of human history.

Before the Neolithic Revolution, humans roamed the earth, following the seasons and the game they hunted. This all changed around 10,000 BCE when our ancestors discovered the magic of agriculture. Miraculously, one could plant a seed from within a plant that you eat into the ground, and another whole plant would grow. This wasn't just a change in how we got our food—it was a revolution that altered every aspect of human life!

We went from wandering bands to bustling villages and eventually to the magnificent cities we know today. This shift from nomadism to putting roots down laid the foundation for everything that followed that we now consider to be human culture and civilization, from art to politics to the way we celebrate and connect.

The discovery and practice of agriculture were at the heart of this monumental shift. With the ability to cultivate crops and domesticate animals, humans no longer needed to constantly move in search of food. They could settle in one place, store surplus food, and build permanent homes. This stability led to the development of towns and cities, the stratification of societies, the specialization of labor, and the creation of complex social and political structures. It also gave rise to new forms of art, architecture, and technology.

One of the most significant impacts of this shift was the way it changed human interactions and the structure of communities. In nomadic societies, social groups were typically small, consisting of extended families or small bands that moved together in search of food. These groups were relatively egalitarian, with decisions made collectively. However, settled societies could support larger populations, leading to the emergence of more hierarchical social structures. Chiefs, priests, and other leaders began to play more prominent roles in organizing and directing communal activities, including rituals.

Settling Down:
The Birth of Complex Rituals

Before the advent of agriculture, rituals in hunter-gatherer societies were intimately tied to the rhythms of nature and the necessities of survival. These early rituals often revolved around the cycles of the moon, the changing seasons, and the migrations of animals. They were performed to ensure successful hunts, to seek protection from natural disasters, and to maintain harmony with the spirits believed to inhabit the natural world.

We can see an example of hunter-gatherer ritual activity still today in the San people of southern Africa, also known as the Bushmen, who have lived as hunter-gatherers for thousands of years, relying on hunting wild animals and gathering wild plants for their sustenance. The San people have a rich cultural heritage and extensive knowledge of their natural environment, which has enabled them to survive in the harsh conditions of the Kalahari Desert and surrounding regions.

They have a rich tradition of trance dances performed to heal the sick, ward off evil spirits, and bring rain. These dances, accompanied by rhythmic clapping and singing, are communal events that reinforce social bonds and shared cultural beliefs.

With the establishment of permanent settlements, the nature of rituals evolved significantly. The predictability of agricultural life allowed for the development of more elaborate and structured rituals. These rituals became central to the social and religious life of early settled societies, marking significant events such as planting and harvest seasons, births, deaths, and marriages.

One of the earliest known settled societies is Çatalhöyük, located in modern-day Turkey, which dates back to around 7500 BCE. Archaeological evidence from this site reveals a complex society with well-developed rituals.

The inhabitants of Çatalhöyük built shrines in their homes, decorated with murals, sculptures, and other artifacts, which suggest ritualistic activities centered around fertility, death, and the veneration of ancestors. The presence of bull horns and goddess figurines indicates that these rituals may have involved animal sacrifices and worship of fertility deities.

In contrast to the simpler rituals of nomadic hunter-gatherers, the rituals of settled societies like Çatalhöyük were more formalized and often required specialized knowledge or roles, such as priests or shamans. These rituals served not only to ensure agricultural success but also to reinforce social hierarchies and communal identities.

The Importance of Rituals
in Human Evolution

Rituals in early settled societies served as the glue that held communities together, reinforcing social cohesion and solidifying group identity. Shared myths and narratives, often revolving around agricultural deities or ancestral spirits, provided a collective understanding of the world and a common heritage to which individuals could anchor their sense of belonging.

Seasonal and harvest festivals became significant events that marked the passage of time, celebrated the fruits of communal labor, and underscored society's reliance on nature's cyclical patterns.

For instance, the ancient Mesopotamians celebrated the Akitu festival, which marked the New Year and the sowing of barley. This festival involved processions, feasts, and the re-enactment of myths, such as the marriage of the god Marduk and the goddess Ishtar. These rituals not only ensured agricultural fertility but also reinforced the social and political order, as the king played a central role in the ceremonies, emphasizing his divine mandate to rule.

As trade between different groups became more common, trade ceremonies emerged, formalizing the exchange of goods and fostering trust and partnership. The symbolic nature of rituals in maintaining social order and transmitting cultural values cannot be overstated. Through ritualistic acts, societies articulated values, norms, and expectations, creating a shared framework for acceptable behavior. Conflict resolution often took a ritualistic form, with established procedures for atonement, reconciliation, and the restoration of harmony – all done under the watchful gaze of the gathered people's deities. The enactment of these rituals provided a platform for airing grievances and settling disputes without resorting to violence, thus preserving the societal fabric.

In early agricultural societies, every event and festival was steeped in religious significance, interwoven with the myths and beliefs that defined the community's worldview. The rhythm of daily life and the cycle of the seasons were orchestrated by deeply held spiritual convictions.

Guided by priests or shamans and under the authority of the king, these societies saw their religious leaders as vital intermediaries between the earthly and the divine. The planting of seeds, the harvest, and the changing of seasons were occasions for elaborate rituals invoking the favor of the gods.

Festivals were grand affairs, with processions, sacrifices, and communal feasts that reaffirmed the sacred order. The priests chanted prayers and conducted ceremonies, while the king, often considered semi-divine, presided over these events, reinforcing his divine right to rule. These gatherings were not just celebrations; they were essential acts of devotion that ensured the prosperity and stability of the community, highlighting the profound connection between religion, leadership, and the social cohesion provided by these early events.

The First Festivals: Early Examples of Organized Events

As anyone who has done extensive traveling knows, it is difficult to stick to a schedule while always on the move. Likewise, the establishment of permanent settlements and the intimate connection with the agricultural cycle and seasons necessitated the creation and observance of periodic events to mark important times in that cycle.

These festivals were linked to equinoxes, solstices, and cross-quarters, as well as the planting and harvesting of crops, reflecting the deep connection between human societies and the natural world. These events tied these societies together through deep shared experiences of myth, ritual, guidance by the priest class, and obedience to the royalty.

For example, the ancient Egyptians celebrated the Festival of Opet, which was held annually in Thebes to honor the gods Amun, Mut, and Khonsu and to ensure the fertility of the land. Sacred statues of these deities were paraded from their shrines in the Karnak Temple to the Luxor Temple, approximately two miles away. The festival, which lasted for nearly a month, was a vibrant blend of religious devotion, communal celebration, and royal propaganda.

If you were an Egyptian in the year 1500 BCE, the streets of Thebes would be alive with anticipation, filled with the scent of incense and the sounds of music. The procession of the gods was a magnificent spectacle. Priests, adorned in elaborate robes, carried the sacred statues on beautifully decorated barques, or ceremonial boats, mounted on their shoulders. These processions were accompanied by musicians playing flutes, harps, and drums, and dancers performing intricate routines. As an observer, you would see the Pharaoh himself participating, reinforcing his divine status and role as the intermediary between the gods and the people.

The air would be thick with a sense of reverence and joy. Along the route, offerings of food and drink would be made, and people would gather to feast together, sharing in the communal bounty. The festival served not only as a religious observance but also as a reaffirmation of social order and the Pharaoh's god-given authority. It was an event that highlighted the deeply ritualistic nature of Egyptian society, where every aspect of life was intertwined with religious practice.

In ancient Greece, the Eleusinian Mysteries were celebrated in honor of Demeter, the goddess of agriculture, and her daughter Persephone. These mysteries, held in the town of Eleusis near Athens, were among the most important religious events in the Greek calendar and were shrouded in secrecy. They symbolized the cycle of life and death, mirroring the seasonal cycle of planting and harvest. To attend the Eleusinian Mysteries was to embark on a profound spiritual journey.

The festival began with a procession from Athens to Eleusis, where participants carried sacred objects and sang hymns. Upon arrival, the initiates underwent purification rituals, bathing in the sea and making offerings to Demeter. The ceremonies themselves included dramatic reenactments of the myth of Demeter and Persephone, symbolizing Persephone's descent into the underworld and her eventual return, which heralded the renewal of life and fertility. The initiation rites, held at night within the Telesterion, a grand hall, involved the sharing of sacred knowledge and visions that were said to profoundly transform the initiates. Participants would witness the symbolic sowing of seeds and the presentation of holy relics while priests and priestesses guided them through the rites. The Mysteries culminated in a great feast and celebration, emphasizing the themes of death and rebirth and promising a blessed afterlife for those initiated.

The Festival of Opet showcased the power and divinity of the Pharaoh, binding the people to their ruler through shared religious experience and communal celebration. While the Eleusinian Mysteries offered a transformative spiritual journey that underscored the importance of agricultural cycles and the promise of renewal and continuity, vital to a society that depended on the land. In both cases, these festivals served as pivotal events that shaped the cultural and social landscape of their respective societies.

They were early examples of how events and gatherings could create a shared sense of identity and purpose, themes that are central to the evolution of human civilization and the development of complex societies. These ancient rituals laid the groundwork for the types of organized events we see today, where cultural, religious, and social functions are celebrated and reinforced through communal participation and shared experience.

The Timeless Nature of Rituals

One may look at these festivals from the dim past and think them strange and inscrutable. But I believe that if you examine our modern events with fresh eyes, you will see that they aren't as different as you might first assume. In fact, all the same elements are present – only the details have changed.

Consider how many of our major celebrations are held at the same time each year, aligning with certain solar cycles or seasons, much like ancient festivals that marked solstices or harvest times. We continue to revere political figures and celebrities, treating them as modern royalty, and events often feature charismatic leaders or speakers who take on a shamanistic role, guiding the collective experience. Music and dancing remain central to creating an atmosphere of fun and celebration, just as they did thousands of years ago.

The use of mind-altering substances, such as alcohol, to foster relaxation and break down the inhibitions of daily life is a tradition that stretches back to the earliest human gatherings. We still come together to watch performances and films, sharing in a collective narrative or myth that entertains and educates. And let's not forget the shared feast – whether it's a holiday dinner, a festival food fair, or a corporate banquet, the act of eating together continues to be a profound way to build community and celebrate our shared humanity.

In essence, the core structure of our events has remained remarkably consistent throughout the ages. The rituals, the communal activities, the roles of individuals within the event, and the underlying purposes – be they to celebrate, to honor, to remember, or to connect – have all stood the test of time. Our modern festivals and gatherings are echoes of our ancestors' celebrations, adapted to fit the cultural context of our times. So, when you attend your next event, think of it as part of a long, unbroken chain of human tradition, stretching back to those ancient days when our forebears gathered under the same sky.

The legacy of the first settled societies is still reflected in our modern events and societies. The structure and purpose of ancient rituals can be seen in contemporary practices, from annual conferences and trade shows to seasonal festivals and cultural celebrations. These events continue to serve as platforms for socialization, knowledge exchange, and the reinforcement of communal values and identities.

The significance of these ritualistic events was starkly highlighted during the COVID-19 pandemic. Despite unprecedented challenges, the desire to adhere to the calendar and maintain the ritual was palpable. For many, these exhibitions were not just business opportunities; they symbolized normalcy and hope in uncertain times.

Rituals, whether in ancient tribal ceremonies or modern-day exhibitions, fulfill a fundamental human need. They offer stability in an ever-changing world, provide a sense of identity, and, most importantly, connect us to our roots, reminding us of our shared human journey. As we continue to innovate and redefine our gatherings, it is essential to recognize and cherish this timeless element that has and will continue to bind us together. Our ability to believe in shared myths and stories has been our strength. In the world of events, rituals are those shared stories—timeless in their essence and profound in their impact.

We have now seen how the shift from nomadic hunter-gatherers to settled agricultural societies brought a fundamental change to human life and that regular ritualistic events were central to this shift. In the next chapter, we will move the clock forward a little closer to the current times to explore the significance of the grand events and spectacles of some of our most powerful ancient societies and reflect on what they can teach us about the present and future of events.

CHAPTER 03

Ancient Civilizations: Events as Spectacles

We now follow the thread of human civilization to the great and powerful ancient civilizations of Egypt, Greece, Rome, and the Far East. In Athens, the grand theaters echo the profound dramas of Sophocles, and the Olympic Games unite rival city-states in peaceful competition.

The awe-inspiring splendor of ancient Egypt is evident during the Festival of Opet, transforming Thebes into a living tableau of divine processions, reinforcing the Pharaoh's godlike authority.

In ancient Rome, the Colosseum roars with the fervor of gladiatorial combat, while chariot races at the Circus Maximus captivate the masses, showcasing the emperor's might and the empire's unity. Meanwhile, the Silk Road connects East and West, bustling with vibrant markets that are not merely places of trade but dynamic centers of cultural exchange, where ideas, stories, and traditions intertwine.

These civilizations, through their magnificent events and gatherings, demonstrate the profound power of communal experiences to shape society, forge identities, and leave an indelible mark on history. The early agricultural settled societies gradually evolved into these great city-states and empires, where events were not just simple gatherings but critical and opulent displays of divine royal authority, political power, military might, intellectual sophistication, and cultural exchange. These events became more elaborate and institutionalized, reflecting the complexity and grandeur of the civilizations themselves. Festivals, athletic competitions, religious ceremonies, and markets were meticulously organized to serve multiple purposes: reinforcing social hierarchies, displaying wealth and power, and fostering unity and cultural exchange.

The evolution from small, settled communities to powerful empires underscores the enduring significance of events in human history, as they became key to the development and expression of civilization itself.

Egyptian Feasts:
Display of Wealth and Power

Let's start our journey in ancient Egypt, where the Pharaohs ruled with divine authority, and their grand feasts were a testament to their wealth and power. The Sed Festival, also known as the Heb-Sed Festival, was one of ancient Egypt's most significant and elaborate royal ceremonies, celebrated to rejuvenate the Pharaoh's strength and reaffirm his divine authority.

Typically held after thirty years of a Pharaoh's reign and then every three years thereafter, the festival was a grand testament to the enduring power and vitality of the ruler. Imagine being in the midst of this magnificent celebration, where the air is thick with incense and the rhythmic beat of drums echoes through the crowd, gathered in awe of their living god.

As a participant or observer, you would witness the Pharaoh, adorned in splendid regalia, performing a series of rigorous physical feats to demonstrate his continued vigor and capability to rule. These activities included running a course, which symbolized his ability to govern the vast land of Egypt, and shooting arrows to display his martial prowess.

The Pharaoh would also participate in rituals that involved the symbolic renewal of his power, such as the donning of a dual crown representing Upper and Lower Egypt, signifying the unification and stability of the nation. Temples and open spaces would be filled with the sights and sounds of jubilation, from lavish feasts to elaborate dances, all in honor of the Pharaoh's eternal strength and the gods' favor.

The significance of the Sed Festival in Egyptian society was profound. It was not merely a celebration of the Pharaoh's longevity but a critical ritual to ensure the continued prosperity and stability of the entire kingdom. The festival reinforced the divine nature of the Pharaoh's rule, reminding the people of his gods-given right to lead. It served as a powerful political tool, showcasing the ruler's undiminished vitality and capability, thereby quelling any doubts or potential unrest among the populace.

Furthermore, the Sed Festival was a renewal of the social contract between the Pharaoh and his subjects, a ceremonial reaffirmation that he would continue to provide order, justice, and abundance under the watchful eyes of the gods. This event was a cornerstone in maintaining the societal and cosmic harmony that the ancient Egyptians so deeply valued.

Greek Theaters & The Origin of the Olympics

Next, we move to ancient Greece, where the open-air theaters were the beating heart of intellectual and democratic life. The Greeks believed in the power of theater to educate, entertain, and bring communities together. Imagine sitting in the stone seats of the Theater of Dionysus in Athens, watching a tragedy by Sophocles or a comedy by Aristophanes unfold on the stage. These performances were more than just entertainment; they were deeply intertwined with the democratic values of the city-state.

In the city of Dionysia, a festival held in honor of the god Dionysus featured dramatic competitions where playwrights presented their works. Citizens gathered to watch these plays, which often explored themes of morality, politics, and human nature. The theater was a space where ideas were exchanged and societal issues were debated, reflecting the intellectual spirit of Greek civilization.

Greek theaters were architectural marvels designed to enhance acoustics and provide a communal viewing experience. The semi-circular design of the theater, with its rising tiers of stone seats, allowed thousands of spectators to witness the performances. The plays themselves were rich with symbolism and often incorporated elements of Greek mythology, reflecting the cultural values and beliefs of the society.

One of the most enduring legacies of ancient Greek culture is the Olympic Games. Originating in 776 BCE in Olympia, these games were held every four years and attracted athletes from all over the Greek world. The Olympics were more than just athletic competitions; they were religious festivals held in honor of Zeus, featuring sacrifices, feasts, and various cultural events.

Athletes competed in events such as running, wrestling, boxing, and chariot racing, vying for glory and the honor of their city-states. Victors were celebrated as heroes, and their achievements were immortalized in statues and songs. The Olympics fostered a sense of unity and shared identity among the often-warring Greek city-states, showcasing the potential for peaceful competition.

The revival of the Olympic Games in the modern era, beginning in 1896, continues this ancient tradition. Today, the Olympics are a global phenomenon, symbolizing the ideals of peace, friendship, and international cooperation.

Roman Extravaganzas: Power and Entertainment

Now, let's step into ancient Rome, where events were spectacles of power and entertainment on an unprecedented scale. The Romans understood the importance of keeping the populace entertained and content, a concept encapsulated in the phrase panem et circenses, meaning "bread and circuses." The roar of the crowd in the Colosseum would have been deafening as gladiators fought for their lives, as would have the cheers that accompanied chariot races in the Circus Maximus.

The Roman games, or ludi, were state-sponsored festivals that included everything from athletic competitions to dramatic performances. The most famous of these were the gladiatorial games, which were both brutal and mesmerizing. These events were not just about bloodshed; they were about showcasing the might and generosity of the emperor, reinforcing his position as the ultimate authority.

The Colosseum, an architectural wonder, could hold up to 80,000 spectators and was equipped with complex machinery to stage elaborate spectacles such as gladiatorial combats, animal hunts, and dramatic reenactments of famous battles. Gladiators, often slaves or prisoners of war, fought not just for survival but also for glory, becoming celebrities in their own right. These games were a tool of political propaganda, demonstrating the emperor's control over life and death and his ability to provide for the people.

The legacy of the Colosseum and the grand spectacles of ancient Rome have left an indelible mark on the way we organize and celebrate modern events. The Colosseum, with its massive scale and architectural ingenuity, was a marvel of its time.

This concept of large-scale entertainment has transcended centuries, influencing our modern arenas and stadiums where thousands gather to watch sports, concerts, and theatrical performances. The spectacle of the Roman games, with their blend of drama, excitement, and communal participation, finds echoes in contemporary events like the Super Bowl, UFC matches, and World Cup tournaments, where the combination of competition, pageantry, and mass entertainment captivates global audiences.

Moreover, the organizational aspects of Roman festivals, including meticulous planning, public engagement, and the use of events to display political power and societal values, continue to resonate today. Just as Roman emperors used grand games to reinforce their authority and connect with the populace, modern leaders and corporations often used major events and public celebrations to shape public perception and foster a sense of unity and identity. The traditions of processions, parades, and ceremonial openings, seen in events ranging from presidential inaugurations to corporate product launches, draw directly from the grandeur of Roman public spectacles.

The Silk Road: Cultural Exchange and Connectivity

Traveling further eastward, we find the Silk Road, the ancient trade route system that connected the East and West. These routes were more than just pathways for goods; they were conduits for cultural exchange and connectivity. A traveler on that way would see thousands upon thousands of caravans laden with silk, spices, and precious metals making their way from China to the Mediterranean, stopping at bustling market cities along the way.

In these market cities, merchants from diverse cultures met and exchanged not only goods but also ideas, stories, and traditions. Events such as fairs and markets along the Silk Roads were vibrant gatherings that facilitated the flow of knowledge and fostered connections between distant civilizations. They were the precursors to modern international trade shows and conventions, emphasizing the timeless importance of cultural and economic exchange.

Traveling the Silk Road in ancient times would have been a sensory feast and a thrilling adventure, an odyssey across vast, diverse landscapes from the bustling markets of Chang'an in China to the grand bazaars of Samarkand and the vibrant ports of Antioch. As you traverse the winding, dusty paths, you encounter a rich tapestry of cultures and peoples, each town and city a unique mosaic of sights, sounds, and smells. Imagine stepping into a bustling caravanserai, the air filled with the mingling aromas of exotic spices and the hum of merchants bartering over silk, jewels, and precious artifacts.

In Samarkand, you might witness the grand Nawruz festival, celebrating the Persian New Year with music, dance, and feasting, where traders from distant lands share stories and traditions. At each stop, you're greeted with the warmth and hospitality of locals eager to exchange goods and tales, offering glimpses into their lives and customs. The Silk

Road is not just a trade route but a vibrant conduit of cultural exchange, where every interaction is an opportunity to experience the wonders of different civilizations and participate in the grand, ongoing story of human connection. Nowadays, our global interconnected world mirrors the Silk Road, as we continuously share and exchange cultures, ideas, and innovations across borders, creating a rich and dynamic global community.

The Enduring Power of Ancient Spectacles

The legacy of these ancient events is still very much evident in our modern societies. The structure and grandeur of Egyptian feasts, Greek theaters and sporting events, Roman spectacles, and Silk Road markets have descended to us today in our contemporary celebrations, performances, and trade fairs. We see echoes of these ancient gatherings in today's grand state functions, theatrical festivals, and global trade expos.

The Olympic Games, revived in modern times, are a direct descendant of the ancient Greek athletic competitions. Similarly, the concept of international expos and world fairs can trace their roots back to the bustling trade hubs of the Silk Roads. These events continue to serve as platforms for showcasing human achievement, fostering international collaboration, and celebrating cultural diversity.

As we reflect on these grand spectacles of ancient civilizations, it becomes clear that events have always been powerful tools for shaping societies. They can unite people, convey cultural values, and reinforce social structures. The passion and creativity that went into organizing these ancient events continue to inspire us today.

In the next chapter, we will explore how the traditions of the Middle Ages further developed these concepts, leading to the vibrant fairs, festivals, and tournaments that characterized this fascinating period in history. Our journey through the history of human gatherings continues, revealing the enduring importance of coming together to celebrate, connect, and innovate.

CHAPTER 04

The Middle Ages: Pilgrimages, Fairs, and Festivals

In the year 1325, Thomas, a young pilgrim from a small village in northern England, has embarked on a journey through the rolling hills and dense forests of medieval Europe. His destination is the bustling market town of Chartres in France, known for its grand cathedral and vibrant fairs. This particular fair is being held to celebrate the Feast of Saint John, a significant religious occasion. The Bishop of Chartres, seeking to honor the saint and promote the town's prosperity, has organized this event, drawing people from all corners of Europe.

As Thomas approaches Chartres, the sounds of music and the scent of roasting meats greet him from a distance, and the vibrant colors of banners and tents fill the air. The hum of the crowd grows louder, and Thomas sees merchants from distant lands displaying their exotic wares, jugglers and musicians entertaining the masses, and knights in shining armor preparing for a grand tournament. This is a medieval fair, a confluence of trade, entertainment, and religious devotion. Pilgrims from all walks of life, driven by faith and the promise of adventure, converge on this lively hub, their long journey through hardship a testament to their piety.

As Thomas navigates through the throng, he finds himself amidst a sea of people, jostling and bustling in the narrow, muddy streets. The fair is alive with the clamor of hawkers shouting their wares, children darting between stalls, and the occasional bray of livestock.

The ground beneath his feet is a mixture of straw and muck, showing the thousands of feet that have trodden this path before him. It is dirty and crowded, with the stench of unwashed bodies mingling with the more pleasant aromas of cooked food and fresh produce.

Despite the chaos, Thomas is captivated by the sights around him. He marvels at the exotic spices from the East, the rich fabrics from Italy, and the intricate jewelry crafted by skilled artisans. He stops to watch a puppet show, laughing with children as the puppets perform comical antics. Nearby, a minstrel strums a lute, singing ballads that tell tales of heroic knights and fair maidens.

The air is thick with excitement and the mingling scents of spices and fresh bread. However, the fair is not without its dangers. Pickpockets lurk in the crowd, eyeing the unsuspecting pilgrims and merchants alike. Fights occasionally break out, fueled by too much ale and the tensions of so many people packed into a small space.

Thomas keeps a close eye on his meager belongings, aware that losing them would mean hardship on his journey. Finding food and shelter is a challenge for a poor pilgrim like Thomas. He relies on the generosity of local churches and monasteries, where he can often find a place to sleep on the floor and a simple meal of bread and soup. On good days, he might afford a hot meal from a vendor—a rare treat of roasted meat or a savory pie. At night, he seeks refuge in the communal areas provided for travelers, sharing stories and warmth with fellow pilgrims.

Despite the hardships, the fair is a place of wonder and opportunity. Thomas participates in a candlelit procession to the cathedral, his spirit lifted by the collective faith and the grandeur of the occasion. The experience is transformative for him, a stark contrast to his quiet village life. At this event, he is inspired to expand his horizons, he has tried new foods, heard new stories and songs, met people from new lands, and learned new skills. And when he returns to his small village, he will bring what he has experienced with him.

When Thomas finally returns to his small village, he is no longer the timid and inexperienced young farmer who left months earlier. His time at the fair in Chartres has enriched his mind and spirit, and he brings back more than just memories. He carries with him new ideas, knowledge, and hopes for the future of his community.

During his time at the fair, Thomas had contracted a debilitating fever, likely brought on by the exhaustion and harsh conditions of the journey. While wandering feverishly through the market, a local herbalist had come to his aid, offering him an herbal infusion that restored his strength within hours. Thomas had carefully watched the woman prepare the remedy, learning that a mixture of sage, mint, and yarrow leaves was effective against fever.

Once back in his village, he brought with him the knowledge of these healing herbs, previously unknown to his people. He began cultivating them in his small family garden and shared the remedy with his neighbors. Soon, the small community came to rely on Thomas and his curative herbs, reducing mortality during seasonal outbreaks and improving the overall quality of life.

The Role of Pilgrimages: Spiritual Journeys

During the Middle Ages, pilgrimages were profound spiritual journeys that shaped both individual lives and societal norms. These pilgrimages were acts of faith, driven by a deep spiritual devotion that compelled individuals to leave the comfort of their homes and undertake arduous journeys to sacred sites.

Imagine the anticipation and trepidation as pilgrims set out, their hearts full of hope and reverence, braving treacherous paths and uncertain whether to reach destinations like Jerusalem, Mecca, Santiago de Compostela, and Canterbury.

These journeys were more than mere travel tourism to check off destinations; they were communal experiences that forged bonds among the pilgrims who traveled together while sharing stories, hardships, and moments of spiritual awakening. Along the way, they stopped at inns, monasteries, and shrines, where they found hospitality and spiritual guidance. These temporary communities, united by a shared purpose, mirrored the networking and camaraderie found in modern trade shows or global product launches, where participants are bound by their shared passion and commitment to their field.

Pilgrimages also had significant economic impacts, as towns along popular routes flourished by providing services to travelers. Markets sprang up to cater to the needs of pilgrims, offering everything from food and lodging to souvenirs and religious relics. The influx of pilgrims stimulated local economies, creating a symbiotic relationship between the travelers and the towns they passed through.

Medieval Fairs: Economic and Social Hubs

Medieval fairs were vibrant, multifaceted events that acted as the beating heart of medieval economic and social life. These fairs were grand social and economic melting pots, drawing people from far and wide to engage in trade, entertainment, and communal activities.

The bustling streets would have been filled with merchants hawking their goods, from exotic spices and textiles to local crafts and produce, and the air alive with the sounds of haggling, laughter, and the clinking of coins as deals are struck and friendships are forged.

Merchants from distant lands brought rare and valuable items, creating a vibrant atmosphere of trade and exchange. The fairs were also places for entertainment, with jugglers, musicians, and performers captivating the crowds. These events provided a platform for innovation display, networking, and significant business deals, much like today's global fairs.

The excitement of a medieval fair was palpable, with colorful tents lining the streets and the air filled with the scent of roasting meats and fresh bread. People of all ages and social standings mingled, creating a unique opportunity for social interaction and cultural exchange. These fairs were crucial in promoting economic growth and social cohesion, much like modern trade shows and industry conventions where companies and professionals convene to showcase innovations, discuss trends, and secure business deals, re-establishing their place within the industry community.

Festivals and Tournaments: Social Order and Celebration

Similar to fairs, festivals and tournaments in the Middle Ages were grand celebrations that served to reinforce social order and provide much-needed entertainment. These events were deeply embedded in the cultural fabric of medieval society, offering a respite from the rigors of daily life and an opportunity for communities to come together in celebration.

It would have been quite a spectacle to watch knights in shining armor competing in jousting tournaments and showcasing their martial skills in melee combat, their lances clashing with a thunderous roar as the crowd cheered on their favorites and jeered at those they disliked.

The pageantry and splendor of these tournaments reinforced the ideals of chivalry and valor, with knights striving to demonstrate their bravery and skill. The tournaments also provided a platform for nobles to display their wealth and status, reinforcing social hierarchies and establishing their authority.

Festivals often coincided with significant religious or agricultural dates, incorporating rituals, feasts, and communal activities that strengthened the bonds within the community. These events were marked by processions, music, dancing, and feasting, creating a sense of unity and shared purpose. The ceremonial aspects of these festivals, such as the blessing of the harvest or the crowning of the May Queen, reinforced social norms and provided a sense of continuity and stability.

Parallels with Modern Events

In today's context, medieval gatherings hold significant parallels with modern exhibitions and industry events. Attendees meticulously plan and prepare for their journeys, understanding their objectives—be it learning, finding new ideas and new products, networking, or expanding business frontiers, and all the other constellations of different needs that only an "in-person" live event can guarantee to reach.

The fairs' bustling energy is replicated in today's industry conventions, exhibitions, and large events, where companies and professionals convene in these global hubs to showcase innovations, discuss trends, and secure business deals, re-establishing their place within the industry community while connecting human to human.

Moreover, the spectacle and pageantry of medieval festivals find their counterparts in keynote speeches, launch events, and award ceremonies, blending celebration, competition, and hierarchy establishment. The COVID-19 pandemic underscored the importance of these events as industries worldwide missed the annual congregation opportunities and the constellation of activities that only happened there. This disruption highlighted our reliance on such gatherings for maintaining economic stability, industry trends, and fundamentally, our collective identity.

Just like in medieval times, a plague may disrupt the calendar of events and the way people meet, but quickly, the people return to their social functions as soon as they can because it is at the base of our life and human evolution.

Our exploration of medieval societal structures provides profound insights into modern gatherings. The Middle Ages were a time when communal identity was all-important, with each pilgrimage, fair, and festival contributing to the societal tapestry.

These gatherings have evolved, but their core purpose remains entrenched in the human experience: the yearning for connection, the pursuit of common goals, and the continual shaping of our collective identity. As we forge ahead, these historical insights are not just intriguing—they are essential blueprints for maintaining the human touch within our ever-evolving societal frameworks.

By understanding the rich heritage of medieval events, we gain a deeper appreciation for the complexity and continuity of human gatherings. Whether through spiritual pilgrimages, bustling fairs, or grand festivals, the Middle Ages laid the groundwork for the sophisticated and diverse events we enjoy today. These historical events remind us that at the heart of every gathering is a desire to connect, celebrate, and create shared experiences that bind us together as a community

From the Renaissance to the Industrial Revolution: Approaching the Modern Event Experience

To walk into a grand palazzo in Florence in 1502 during the height of the Renaissance would have been to experience a living history. The room is filled with the soft glow of candlelight, and the air buzzes with the excitement of intellectual exchange. Around the room, you see some of the most brilliant minds of the era A fifty-year-old Leonardo da Vinci passionately discussing his latest inventions, a young Michelangelo displaying his sculptures of the human form, and Niccol Machiavelli in his early thirties debating politics with fervor.

Picture being a fly on the wall as Galileo Galilei unveils his latest astronomical discoveries, challenging the established order and igniting debates that will reverberate for centuries. The atmosphere is electric with creativity and intellectual daring.

This is a Renaissance salon, a gathering of artists, scientists, and thinkers sharing ideas that will soon change the world. These gatherings were hotbeds of innovation where foundations of modern science, art, and philosophy were established. These salons, hosted by wealthy patrons like the de Medici family, were the lifeblood of Renaissance culture, providing a space where knowledge was shared and revolutionary ideas took flight. They represent the early stages of the modern conference or symposium, where the exchange of groundbreaking ideas is celebrated and fostered.

Renaissance Intellectual Salons and Gatherings

The Renaissance was a period of extraordinary intellectual and artistic awakening, and at its core were the intellectual salons and gatherings that became the epicenters of innovation. Renaissance salons emerged during the 15th and 16th centuries in Italy, particularly in cities like Florence, Venice, and Rome.

These gatherings were influenced by the earlier medieval courts and the humanist movement, which emphasized the revival of classical knowledge and the promotion of intellectual and artistic endeavors.

Salons were typically hosted by wealthy and influential patrons, often women of high social standing, known as salonnières. These patrons provided a space for intellectuals, artists, scientists, and writers to come together and share ideas. Notable salonnières included Isabella d'Este, a prominent patron of the arts, and Elisabetta Gonzaga. The attendees of Renaissance salons were a mix of scholars, poets, artists, musicians, and philosophers, along with their wealthy patrons.

The atmosphere of a Renaissance salon was both formal and convivial. Held in grand palazzos or opulent chambers, salons were adorned with artworks, sculptures, and luxurious furnishings. The settings were designed to inspire and stimulate creativity and discourse. The settings inspired lively discussions, with artists, scientists, and philosophers exchanging ideas and challenging each other's perspectives. These salons were incubators of progress, where the works of Leonardo da Vinci, Michelangelo, and Galileo Galilei were not only discussed but also influenced and refined through collective scrutiny and support. The energy in these rooms would have been palpable as attendees passionately debated topics ranging from human anatomy to celestial mechanics, laying the groundwork for the scientific revolution and the birth of modern humanism.

The Legacy of Renaissance Salons Today

By the late 16th century, the nature of salons began to change with the rise of academies and scientific societies. However, the legacy of Renaissance salons endured, influencing the development of the Enlightenment salons in 18th-century France and beyond.

The salons played a pivotal role in the cultural and intellectual life of the period, facilitating the exchange of ideas across disciplines and contributing significantly to the advancements of the Renaissance. These gatherings promoted humanism by reviving classical learning and emphasizing the potential of human achievement, thereby reinforcing the principles of this intellectual movement.

They also encouraged patronage, allowing artists and scholars to secure financial support from wealthy hosts, which was crucial for the continuation of their work. Furthermore, the interdisciplinary nature of salons fostered innovation, leading to the cross-pollination of ideas and sparking numerous advancements in art, science, and literature. Renaissance salons and modern events share a fundamental essence: they are gatherings where people with shared interests and passions come together to exchange ideas, showcase their creations, and inspire one another.

Just as the intellectuals and artists of the Renaissance gathered in opulent rooms to discuss philosophy, science, and art, today's enthusiasts congregate at conferences, conventions, and expos to delve into topics ranging from technology and science to literature and entertainment.

When tech enthusiasts flock to events like the Consumer Electronics Show (CES) in Las Vegas to explore the latest innovations and engage in thought-provoking discussions, they are a new iteration of Renaissance thinkers debating new philosophical concepts and scientific discoveries.

Similarly, literary festivals today, such as the Hay Festival, mirror the Renaissance salons where poets and writers read their works and received immediate feedback. These modern events continue the tradition of fostering creativity, collaboration, and the dissemination of groundbreaking ideas, highlighting the timeless human desire to connect, learn, and create collectively.

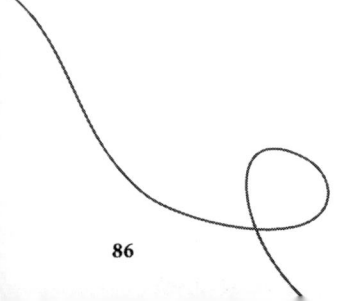

The Dawn of Ticketed Events in an Evolving World

As the Renaissance gave way to the early modern period, the nature of gatherings again began to evolve. The concept of ticketed events emerged, democratizing access to knowledge and entertainment.

Unlike the exclusive Renaissance salons, there were now organized public events where ideas could be disseminated to a wider audience. Theaters like the Globe in London, where Shakespeare's plays were performed, introduced the concept of paying for admission, making cultural experiences accessible to the masses. Similarly, public lectures and scientific demonstrations provided a platform for thinkers like Isaac Newton to share their discoveries with the public, fostering a culture of learning and curiosity that transcended social classes.

Public lectures, scientific demonstrations, and theatrical performances now became accessible to the common man, allowing a broader audience to participate in the cultural and intellectual life of the time. A burgeoning culture of paid performances allowed for a more structured and financially sustainable way to manage attendance and ensure that productions could be funded and maintained.

How the Industrial Revolution Transformed the Logistics and Scale of Events

Following the Renaissance, the nature of events evolved significantly. The Enlightenment period in the 18th century saw the rise of scientific societies and intellectual gatherings, such as the Royal Society in London and the Académie des Sciences in Paris, where scholars and scientists would meet to share their discoveries and advancements.

These gatherings were often formalized and supported by membership fees, laying further groundwork for the concept of ticketed events.

The Industrial Revolution brought about profound changes in the logistics and scale of events through technological advancements such as the steam engine, telegraph, and later the railroad that revolutionized travel and communication, making it possible for people to attend events that were previously out of reach. This era saw the rise of grand exhibitions and world fairs, which showcased the latest industrial achievements and innovations on an unprecedented scale.

One of the most significant events during the Industrial Revolution was the Great Exhibition of 1851, held in London's Crystal Palace. This event was a monumental showcase of industrial design and technology, featuring exhibits from around the world. Organized by Prince Albert and Henry Cole, the Great Exhibition attracted over six million visitors, making it one of the first truly global events. The logistics of organizing such a massive event were made possible by advancements in transportation and communication, highlighting the critical role of technology in shaping modern events.

Another pivotal event was the World's Columbian Exposition in 1893, held in Chicago. Also known as the Chicago

World's Fair, it celebrated the 400th anniversary of Christopher Columbus's arrival in the New World. This exposition was a showcase of architectural, technological, and cultural achievements and drew millions of visitors. It introduced many Americans to the wonders of electricity, including the first-ever Ferris wheel, and marked a turning point in public engagement with technological progress.

Event Accessibility &
The Democratization
of the Event Experience

Key to these large events during the Industrial Revolution was their accessibility. Public transportation systems, such as railways and steamships, made it possible for people from various social strata to attend events that were previously inaccessible.

This democratization of events fostered a more inclusive society, where ideas and innovations could be shared across a broader audience, fueling further progress and development.

The rise of the middle class and increased leisure time also played a significant role in making events more accessible. As people had more disposable income and free time, they sought out cultural and educational experiences, leading to the proliferation of museums, theaters, and public lectures. Events became accessible not only to the elite but also to the general public, creating a more informed and engaged society.

Today, we stand on the shoulders of these historic milestones. Our modern events are deeply rooted in the essence of sharing, inspiring, and co-creating—principles that found their footing in the dynamic world of Renaissance and post-Renaissance Europe. Our roles as event organizers, facilitators, or participants carry forward a legacy that began over half a millennium ago. These gatherings, whether global trade shows or local meetups, echo the humanistic ideals of the Renaissance and the structural pragmatism of the Industrial Revolution.

One event that truly showcases this incredible blend of global reach and local relevance is "AF - Artigiano in Fiera." This unique combination of festival and exhibition brings together over a million visitors each year to celebrate, explore, and trade the finest artisan goods and craftsmanship from around the world. It's a vibrant gathering that captures the essence of cultural exchange and creativity on a grand scale.

Understanding our past offers invaluable insights into our present and future. The evolution of events from the Renaissance to the Industrial Revolution not only provides a glimpse into our journey but also holds a mirror to our societal evolution. As we organize or participate in events today, we are partaking in a historical ritual that has been refined over centuries.

It's a testament to our never-ending quest for collective growth, understanding, and connection—a journey that continues to shape the human experience.

CHAPTER 06

The 20th Century: The Spread of Globalization

As the world was rapidly moving forward in the 20th century, one event encapsulated the dawn of modernity like no other the 1939 New York World's Fair. To walk through the sprawling grounds of Flushing Meadows, surrounded by futuristic pavilions and technological marvels that promised a brighter tomorrow, would have been to be amazed and inspired at the wonders of human progress during a tumultuous time.

The fair introduced television to the masses, unveiled the first public demonstration of fax machines, and even had a robot named Elektro that could walk and talk. This moment marked the beginning of an era where events were not merely regional gatherings but grand spectacles that could influence and inspire an increasingly global populace.

The 20th century was a time of extraordinary transformation, driven by the forces of globalization. Events were central to this massive change as powerful platforms for bringing people together, transcending borders, and fostering a sense of global community. The intertwining of globalization and events created a dynamic relationship, where each drove the other forward, leading to the creation of international spectacles that captivated the world.

While events spurred globalization, globalization expanded the reach and scale of events, allowing them to become truly international in nature. Advances in transportation and communication made it possible for people to travel across continents to attend events. Air travel, in particular, revolutionized the way people experienced global events. For the first time in human history, a person could attend the Summer Olympics in Helsinki, marvel at the Miss Universe pageant in Long Beach, experience the Edinburgh International Festival, and witness the coronation of Queen Elizabeth II in London, all in the summer of 1952.

The Rise of International Expos & Olympic Games

International expos, or world's fairs, became hallmark events of the 20th century, showcasing the latest technological advancements, cultural achievements, and industrial progress from around the globe.

These grand exhibitions were national pride displays and platforms for international collaboration and competition. The 1900 Paris Exposition Universelle, for instance, celebrated the achievements of the 19th century and heralded the innovations of the new century. Attracting over 50 million visitors, it highlighted the growing interconnectedness of the world. Each pavilion at these expos was a miniature world, offering a glimpse into the culture, technology, and aspirations of the participating countries.

From the awe-inspiring Eiffel Tower at the 1889 Paris Expo to the futuristic Space Needle at the 1962 Seattle World's Fair, these events were stages where nations presented their best, inspiring awe and fostering international dialogue and collaboration.

In tandem with international expos, the modern Olympic Games were the other major worldwide event experience. Revived in Athens in 1896 by Pierre de Coubertin, this event marked a significant cultural moment, symbolizing a return to ancient ideals of athletic competition while reigniting historical legacies and fostering a sense of global camaraderie.

Since the revival, events have often been at the center of technological and cultural shifts. The 1912 Stockholm Games were notable for the introduction of electronic timing devices and a public address system, reflecting broader trends in industrial progress and communication. The 1952 games in Helsinki marked the first participation of the Soviet Union and other Eastern Bloc countries, reflecting the growing Cold War tensions. The inclusion of these nations in a global event underscored the Olympics' role in providing a peaceful platform for geopolitical rivals to compete.

Broadcasts of these events reached millions, making them truly global spectacles. The 1964 Tokyo Olympics, for instance, was the first to be broadcast live via satellite, allowing people around the globe to witness the triumphs and tribulations of athletes in real time. The power of events like the Olympics lies in their ability to bring people together, inspire progress, and reflect the broader currents of human history and development.

Events as Economic Drivers

As globalization progressed, events evolved into significant economic drivers. Trade fairs, conventions, and exhibitions became vital platforms for businesses to showcase their products, forge partnerships, and enter new markets. The Canton Fair in China, established in 1957, exemplifies this evolution. It became a crucial event for international trade, bringing together buyers and sellers from around the world.

The fair has become one of the largest and most influential trade fairs in the world, playing a pivotal role in China's economic development and integration into the global market. When the Canton Fair was first established, China was relatively isolated economically. The fair provided a critical platform for international trade, enabling Chinese manufacturers to connect with global buyers. It also facilitated the export of Chinese goods, generating much-needed foreign exchange and helping to develop the nation's manufacturing capabilities.

These large events also generated substantial revenue, created jobs, and stimulated local economies. For example, the 1984 Los Angeles Olympics not only showcased athletic excellence but also revitalized the city as a whole. The games revitalized the city's economy by generating a significant financial surplus through innovative corporate sponsorships and media rights sales while minimizing public spending. The Games created approximately 70,000 jobs, boosted tourism, and led to lasting infrastructure improvements, including upgraded sports facilities and enhanced transportation systems.

This success not only showcased Los Angeles globally but also set a new standard for future large-scale events, emphasizing the importance of private funding and cost-effective planning.

In addition to these tangible benefits, large events leave a profound and lasting "soft legacy." This concept, increasingly studied in recent years, encompasses the long-term social, cultural, and psychological effects on the host city and country. For example, the 2012 London Olympics significantly boosted civic pride and community cohesion, fostering a deep sense of unity and national identity.

Similarly, the 2000 Sydney Olympics enhanced Australia's international reputation and cultural identity, creating a lasting legacy of increased volunteerism and community engagement.

Beyond the economic and infrastructural gains, such events often inspire positive social policies and practices, including better inclusivity and accessibility measures. While the immediate financial impact of these events is undeniable, their soft legacy can be just as powerful, shaping societal attitudes and fostering meaningful, long-term change

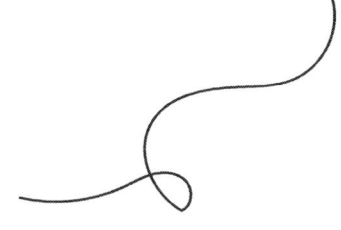

Music Festivals & Political Rallies: Cultural & Political Nexus Points

The 20th century also saw the rise of music festivals and political rallies as significant events with cultural and political impact. Music festivals like Woodstock in 1969 became iconic symbols of cultural movements, bringing together people from diverse backgrounds to celebrate music, peace, and social change. Woodstock was far more than just a concert, it was a cultural milestone that reflected the counterculture movement of the 1960s, influencing music, fashion, and social attitudes in a way that we still experience and remember today.

Political rallies, on the other hand, played a crucial role in shaping public opinion and mobilizing social movements. The Civil Rights March on Washington in 1963, where Martin Luther King Jr. delivered his famous "I Have a Dream" speech, was a pivotal moment in history. This rally brought together hundreds of thousands of people, highlighting the power of collective action and the impact of events in driving social change.

Growth of Corporate Events and Trade Fairs

Growth of Corporate Events and Trade Fairs The corporate world also saw exponential growth in events, particularly B2B exhibitions and trade fairs. These gatherings became epicenters of industry evolution, where the brightest minds and biggest players in various sectors converged. Trade fairs were no longer just marketplaces; they became stages for introducing groundbreaking ideas and forging partnerships that dictated industry trends.

For example, the Consumer Electronics Show (CES), founded in 1967 by the Consumer Technology Association, quickly became the premier event for showcasing groundbreaking technologies. Serving as a global platform, CES has introduced revolutionary products like the VCR, CD player, and HDTV, influencing consumer technology trends worldwide. Its significant economic impact, role in setting industry standards, and ability to raise consumer awareness have made it a pivotal event in driving technological progress and shaping the future of consumer electronics.

These events are meticulously planned and executed, with significant investments in logistics, marketing, and technology. They provide opportunities for businesses to demonstrate their expertise, build brand awareness, and gain a competitive edge. The growth of corporate events has reflected the increasing complexity and interconnectedness of the global economy, emphasizing their role in fostering innovation and economic growth. Moreover, the profound connection between trade fairs and their host cities has led to substantial long-term benefits beyond immediate economic gains. These events, in collaboration with the cities they take place in, provide an enormous boost to their specific niches.

A notable example is the impact of trade fairs on the "Made in Italy" brand. Events such as "Il Salone del Mobile" in Milan have become iconic within the design industry. Milan, now recognized as the world capital of design and fashion, owes much of its status to the annual influx of design professionals, entrepreneurs, and experts attending these events. The Salone del Mobile has drawn hundreds of thousands of industry professionals every year, enhancing the city's reputation and fostering a collaborative environment that has emphasized the strengths of local industrial districts. This synergy between the events and the city's inherent capabilities has significantly boosted the "Made in Italy" concept, establishing it as a benchmark for quality, style, and innovation across various sectors.

Such exhibitions have not only cemented Italy's global standing in design but have also reinforced its excellence in other industries, creating a lasting legacy that transcends the events themselves.

Similarly, the Automechanika trade fair in Frankfurt has played a crucial role in enhancing the global stature of Germany's automotive industry. This event, one of the largest international automotive trade fairs, showcases innovations in vehicle parts, equipment, and services. It has significantly contributed to the exponential growth and importance of the automotive sector in Germany.

Coupled with Germany's robust foundation in car manufacturing and component production, Automechanika has propelled the industry to new heights, reinforcing Germany's position as a global leader in automotive excellence. The synergy between the trade fair and the nation's strong industrial base has created a legacy of innovation and quality that continues to drive the industry's success.

The Media & Internet's Role in Amplifying Events

The role of media in this era cannot be overstated. The 20th century saw the rise of mass media, including newspapers, radio, television, and later, the internet. These platforms transformed how events were covered, consumed, and remembered.

Media coverage amplified the impact of events, extending their reach beyond physical attendees to global audiences. The rise of live broadcasting and real-time reporting created a new dynamic where events could shape public opinion and cultural trends on a massive scale. The media became a powerful tool for storytelling, turning events into center points that captured the imagination of the world.

Every event provides a perfect opportunity to spotlight its theme, not only from an operational and engagement standpoint but also regarding the subject matter itself. For instance, in B2B fairs that are often highly specialized in a particular sector, the attention to that sector becomes pivotal as the event approaches.

The ritual of these events ensures that all stakeholders, including the media and the public, focus intensely on that industry. When an agricultural fair begins, it becomes the moment for the entire ecosystem to engage in debates and discussions—bringing in political, media, and public attention. Events act as catalysts, shining a spotlight on specific themes and industries, thus driving conversation and development around those areas.

At the cusp of the 20th century and the dawn of the 21st century, we experienced the advent of the internet, which revolutionized how events were organized, attended, and experienced. The internet allowed for the rapid dissemination of information, making it easier to promote events and reach a global audience. Online registration, virtual tickets, and live streaming became common, making events more accessible to people regardless of their geographic location, emphasizing even more the importance of being "present" in-person.

Events like TED Conferences capitalized on this technology, offering not just in-person experiences but also making their content available online to millions of viewers. This digital shift enabled events to have a lasting impact, as talks and performances could be accessed long after the event had concluded, fostering a continuous engagement with the audience, but having the opportunity of participating in a live TED conference as a special privilege.

Modern Events Reflecting Historical Ideals

Modern events continue to reflect historical ideals, drawing on the rich traditions of the past while embracing contemporary innovations. The principles of celebration, competition, and community that characterized ancient and medieval gatherings remain central to today's events. Whether it's a music festival, a trade fair, or a political rally, the essence of coming together to share, learn, and celebrate persists.

Today's events are more technologically advanced, yet they are rooted in the same human desire for connection and shared experience. The digital age has introduced new possibilities for virtual and hybrid events, expanding access and engagement. However, the fundamental principles of events remain unchanged, highlighting the timeless nature of human gatherings in person, as the maximum expression of living the serendipity, the opportunity of meeting and fulfilling a constellation of needs that the virtual or pure digital experience cannot match.

The 20th century was a transformative period. Driven by the forces of globalization, technological advancement, and cultural change, events evolved from primarily local and regional gatherings to global phenomena, reflecting and shaping the world's economic, political, and cultural landscape. International expos, large exhibitions, sports games, music festivals, and corporate events became defining features of the century.

The philosophical implications of global events are profound. As events became truly global, they contributed to a collective human consciousness. People began to see themselves as part of a larger world community, fostering a sense of shared destiny and mutual responsibility. This global perspective has the potential to drive collaborative efforts toward solving worldwide challenges, promoting peace, and advancing human progress.

As we conclude this historical journey through events, it is clear that the evolution of gatherings has been a continuous process of adaptation and innovation. The 20th century set the stage for the present and future of events, where the principles of globalization, technological integration, and cultural exchange will continue to drive their development. Understanding the history of events provides valuable insights into their enduring significance and potential to shape our collective future, inspiring us to create events that connect, celebrate, and propel us forward.

THE ART
& SCIENCE
OF EVENT
ORGANIZING

PART 2

CHAPTER 07

Inspiring and Motivating through Events

I don't usually like to talk about myself, as the focus should be on the power of events, but I think that sharing my personal journey as an event organizer may be interesting to the reader.

Events have been the thread running throughout my life, guiding me from a young boy growing up in Italy to a passionate entrepreneur in the event industry. My mother told me that I have been organizing events since I was three years old. It's in my DNA. It seems there was some destiny for me in this field, as I kept being brought back to organizing, studying, and hosting gatherings, no matter where life took me.

My fascination with events began in my childhood. Growing up in a village near Venice, I was surrounded by a family that loved to host gatherings. Our family house, with its extensive gardens, was the backdrop for numerous gatherings. This house, which my grandfather built a beautiful estate, became a hub for countless parties and events, shaping my upbringing and my love for bringing people together.

Events are somehow also related to my family name. In Italy, my extended family, the Gallorini's, have a tradition of hosting the Gallorinata every 2nd of June. This event, held in the mountains close to Florence, where our family originated in the 16th century, is a grand gathering of Gallorini's from all over the world.

Italian culture places great importance on getting together to eat, talk, and enjoy each other's company, and this cultural emphasis on connection and celebration has profoundly influenced me. My family really went all-out for our parties and gatherings we even created an annual "Olmo Trophy" that is awarded each year to the winning team of a sort of mini-Olympic Games in our garden. We also had various cultural events where we performed live music, read poetry, discussed ideas, and cooked together.

My brother was another significant influence on me. He is a black belt when it comes to organizing parties. He loves to meet with people so much that he holds two birthday parties a year for himself, one in the winter and one in the summer, just so he has an excuse to invite friends over to connect and have fun. Watching him masterfully create fun events, I learned that even small gatherings required the same methodologies as large events, sparking my interest in event organization. All these experiences from my family and my childhood were deeply ingrained in my upbringing and instilled in me a profound appreciation for the power of events.

From Academia
to Entrepreneurship

My path initially seemed set towards academia, given my parents' and grandparents' backgrounds as university professors and lecturers. That was the path set out before me. However, while in university, I naturally gravitated towards organizing events and began to explore my passion for organizing them more seriously.

When I went to university in Italy, I was surprised to find that there weren't any fun events that brought the students together.

I said, "Where are the parties? There are no amazing parties!"

So, with my future wife and my best friends, we started a small business called "UNIMIND" organizing events such as disco-parties, Miss University, the Spring event in mid-March, the Autumn event in October, the Winter Christmas party in mid-December, the yearly soccer tournament, and volleyball tournaments all year around. After a few years, we organized the biggest Miss University of the region, with 4,000 people coming from all over the Veneto region to our party. And it became super successful without us even expecting it to be.

Our parties were unique because they started earlier in the evening, a departure from the typical late-night discos of the late 90s and early 2000s. We even provided buses to transport students to the venues for free through working with the local government to avoid the use of cars, emphasizing safety as a high priority.

These events, drawing 3,000 to 4,000 people, were a huge success and made me quite known in the university. We rented entire venues and created unique experiences with themes, music, and even spaghetti "aglio and olio" at midnight! Organizing these events sparked my passion and planted the seed for what would become my career.

My journey took a significant turn when I went to Paris to work for FIAT Automobile while completing my thesis. It was there that I realized I was not cut out for the rigid structure of large corporations. The distance between myself and the company's top management felt insurmountable, and I knew I needed a different path. This realization was crystallized during my work on a thesis project involving new car buyer satisfaction surveys. This project not only introduced me to the world of research but also planted the seed for my future entrepreneurial endeavors.

Returning to Italy, I had the opportunity with my professors to start a company to gather and analyze data for car dealerships. This idea led to the founding of my second business experience after UNIMIND, which quickly evolved into organizing professional events for the automotive industry and founding the company Quintegia in 2004.

One of our most successful initiatives was the Automotive Dealer Day (ADD) in Verona, which became the largest event of its kind in Europe and the second largest in the world. This experience solidified my belief in the transformative power of events.

Working with incredible university professors Leonardo Buzzavo and Giuseppe Volpato as business partners and having the chance to travel and visit the biggest event in the automotive dealer business in Las Vegas every year exposed me to a different way of thinking. The first trip to the United States was my first international business travel experience, and the vibrant culture and the dynamic event business environment were inspiring.

The guidance I received from Professors Buzzavo and Volpato was incredible. That journey was a revelation that led me to realize that I wanted to create something unique and different from what we saw abroad, something that combined the "energy" of the U.S. event and allowed us to see the direct impact of our work. This realization was a driving force behind starting this venture.

I was full of passion for innovation, yet I also focused on the details because I discovered that the beauty is in the details.

The company grew rapidly, and by the age of 30, I was running a multi-million-euro business. However, this success came at a cost. I was living a fast-paced life, always on the move, continuing to study to fulfill my desire to have "university status", all the while running a company, and it eventually caught up with me. This period of intense activity culminated in a serious health scare that forced me to reevaluate my life.

Healing My Illness Through Following My Passion for Events

In January of 2012, as I was leaving my office, I discovered that I could not properly move my right eye! I was so surprised by this that I fell down. After a trip to the doctor, I was diagnosed with Myasthenia Gravis, a rare and debilitating illness that brought my whirlwind life to a halt. "Gravis" in Latin means very severe.

This illness gradually and relentlessly destroys the neurological system, starting from the extremities like fingers and toes, due to the body's inability to produce a specific neurotransmitter called acetylcholine.

However, I always say that I am super lucky, and I have been blessed throughout my life. Even in that scary diagnosis I got lucky again, at that hospital, there was a doctor who specialized in this rare disease.

For most people, Myasthenia Gravis usually starts in the extremities and gradually progresses. However, for me, due to stress and other factors, it manifested differently. Instead of starting in my fingers and toes, it began in my eyes and for this reason the diagnosis went very fast. There are only a few medicines that can treat this disease. One is called "Myasthenia-non" and needs to be taken with a mix of other psychiatric drugs. While it helps, it also severely weakens the body. By February, my condition was critical, because not only was my body weak, but I was also deeply depressed.

At the same time, my wife was eight months pregnant with our first daughter, and my mentor, Professor Volpato, was battling cancer. This period was marked by emotional turmoil. When you are 32 years old and in that phase of life, when you discover that your body doesn't support you, you can get really depressed.

Emma was born on the 18th of March, but I was so weak that I couldn't even hold her. I hit my lowest point of depression. Then, on the 4th of April, my mentor, Professor

Volpato, passed away. These events were life-altering and made me realize that I needed to change my life.

I decided to quit my company, take a step back, and focus on what truly mattered to me. This period of reflection allowed me to reconnect with my passion for events and find a new direction for my career. Despite these hardships, my passion for events provided a lifeline. I found solace and purpose in studying and understanding more about the events industry, which helped me navigate through the darkest times.

During my illness, I had to undergo multiple treatments and challenges. The physical and emotional toll was immense. There were moments of doubt and fear; however, my wife, my brother, my best friends, and my parents, along with my passion for events, kept me going. I realized that organizing events was not just a job or a career, but a calling that gave me purpose and joy. This realization became my guiding light during those challenging times.

The medicine helped me recover. However, the new approach to my life, the strength of my family, and especially my wonderful daughters Emma and Elena played a significant role in my healing. It was a combination of medical treatment and a renewed focus on what truly mattered to me that helped me overcome this challenge. It was the start of a new beginning.

A New Purpose

Today, I am the CEO of a boutique multinational research company that specializes in the event industry called GRS Research & Strategy. Our unique approach and very precise specialization, which focuses on understanding the needs behind the reasons for attending an event (the "why" behind the decision), has led to collaborations with various event companies at the beginning in Italy and quickly, after that, internationally.

This approach emphasizes engaging with the beneficiaries of the event (visitors, exhibitors, sponsors, cities, etc.) to gather valuable insights and create events that are not just operational but strategically impactful and focus on optimization.

Reflecting on my journey, I realize that my passion for events has been a constant thread throughout my life. From organizing small family gatherings to leading major international events, I have always been driven by the desire to connect people and create memorable experiences. Being so fascinated about the final meaning of events, that are by nature in-person. For me, there is nothing more interesting than the deep connection and role of events in mankind's evolution.

Through the unstoppable evolutions of events, my passion is also my mission: to study and discover more and more about the power of collective gatherings to co-create the future.

Somehow I can say that my story is a good example of the power of following one's passion and the transformative impact of events on individuals and communities.

Today, I wake up every morning grateful for the opportunity to do what I love. My company focuses on gathering and analyzing data to improve the event experience for attendees and organizers alike. We are constantly innovating, finding new ways to enhance the value of events and create insights for the organizer through going deeper and deeper into the core reason "why" events exist.

The importance of data in event planning and the legacy of events continue to drive my work and inspire me to create meaningful experiences for others. I hope that my story inspires others to pursue their passions, overcome challenges, and create meaningful connections through events. The journey is not always easy, but it is filled with opportunities for growth, learning, and making a lasting impact.

CHAPTER 08

The Legacy of Events

In a small, dimly lit bedroom in Nigeria, a young woman named Amina sits at her desk, her face illuminated by the soft glow of her computer screen. She clicks a link, and suddenly she's transported into a virtual conference room filled with people from around the world. She is an attendee of an online conference focused on sustainable agriculture and community development two topics close to her heart. As she watches the presentations and participates in the discussions, she feels a sense of connection and inspiration that transcends the miles between her and the other attendees.

Amina listens intently as experts from various fields share their knowledge and experiences. She learns about innovative farming techniques that can thrive in harsh climates, the importance of crop diversity, and the benefits of community-based farming cooperatives. During a breakout session, she engages in a lively discussion with a group of attendees from different countries, exchanging ideas and solutions for common challenges. One presentation, in particular, catches her attention a successful entrepreneur from India shares how he transformed his small village by implementing sustainable practices and creating job opportunities for the locals.

Inspired by the stories and armed with new knowledge, Amina begins to envision a future where she can make a difference in her own community. She starts to dream of creating her own business that not only lifts her family out of poverty but also empowers her neighbors. She imagines a cooperative farm where everyone works together, sharing resources and knowledge to improve their yields and create a sustainable source of income. The conference becomes a turning point in her life, igniting a passion and determination to bring positive change to her region.

When the conference ends, Amina feels a mix of emotions. She is grateful for the opportunity to learn and connect with so many passionate individuals, but she also longs for the day when she can attend such an event in person. The experience has shown her the power of virtual connections, but it has also deepened her appreciation for physical gatherings where people can share their energy and build relationships face-to-face.

The next year, she saved up enough money to fly to Bologna in Italy to *attend the EIMA International, the biggest agricultural exhibition, which she discovered through the online conference. Being there physically opens up a whole new world of opportunity and possibility. Amina passionately attends some conference sessions, taking notes and asking questions. She talks with many of the speakers and fellow attendees as she starts to build a network of mentors and allies who support her vision.*

But the revelation was while she went through the dozens of pavilions at the Bologna exhibition, where she saw the variety and the incredible opportunities given by the new technology. She spoke with as many of the technicians, salespeople, and business owners, as well as anyone else who was there to innovate and create in the field of agriculture.

The serendipity of those moments, the opportunity of sharing ideas, connecting dots, and imagining and dreaming with many other passionate people in the agriculture business was a huge boost for her greater dream, to create value for her community. She even meets another Nigerian, a wealthy businessman who has an interest in agriculture and wants to do something that will truly help his countrymen.

With each in-person meeting, her confidence grows, and she starts to develop a concrete plan for her business. She decides to focus on organic farming, using the techniques she learned and saw in practice in various booths to produce healthy and high-quality crops.

As Amina starts to implement her plans, she faces numerous challenges, but her determination and the support of her new network keep her going, knowing that there is a full industry available to co-create the future with her. Slowly but surely, her dream starts to take shape. With the help of her family, she sets up a small farm, recruits a few dedicated workers, and begins to see the fruits of her labor. The impact on her community is profound.

People are not only earning a better living, but they are also gaining a sense of pride and hope for the future. Amina is now eagerly awaiting the next edition of the EIMA International exhibition so that she can again experience that rituality of excitement, passion, and growth both personally and professionally.

This scene, commonplace today, would have been unimaginable just fifteen years ago. The advent of computers, smartphones, Skype, Zoom, and other technologies has revolutionized the way we connect, allowing us to attend events digitally through video and the internet. Yet, throughout the vast expanse of human history, the only way to truly connect was by being physically present, feeling the warmth of another's handshake, hearing the murmur of the crowd, and sharing the air in a communal space.

Even though we now have the convenience of virtual conferences and digital events, the heart and soul of gatherings remain rooted in the physical world. The essence of events is in the journey, the act of traveling to be together, to experience the energy and the ambiance that only comes from sharing a space with others. These new technologies, rather than replacing the need for physical presence, have highlighted its irreplaceable value. They have made us realize how special and necessary the physical experience is, deepening our appreciation for the moments when we can come together in person to create memories and forge connections that transcend the digital realm.

The Importance of "In-Person"

In the past, the concept of an event occurring in-person was quite obvious. In fact, it was the only way. Today, the prospect of traveling to attend an event in-person can be seen as something people may question. Why should I go through all the hassle of flying in airplanes, getting a visa, paying for a hotel, and leaving the comforts of my daily life and home when I can just purchase a cheaper digital ticket and vicariously experience the event through my laptop screen?

My feeling, and I'm sure about this, is that if we meet with a screen in front of us, we don't feel each other's energy. We miss a lot. It's not just about listening and understanding; we miss the moment, the experience, and being in the same place. When we're together in person, we're fully immersed in our bubble, breathing the same air, feeling the same smells, and hearing the same noises without the screen as an intermediary.

A true event has to be experienced live and in person. Digital tools can empower this experience through all the possible ways of "expanding" our meeting opportunities, such as with the event's cell phone app before, during, and after the show. However, it's the in-person element that makes people truly grasp the future. The physical presence of attendees, the exchange of energy, and the spontaneous interactions that occur in a shared space are irreplaceable.

I feel that the in-person moment is not just two people in the same place at the same time. It's their energy, it's everything that is related. We are physical beings, and we need that kinesthetic and intimate experience of being face-to-face with others in a shared intentional space. It all goes back to what we talked about earlier in this book: how the ritualistic aspect of events is key.

This is why I wanted to write this book: because in-person events are extraordinary and important. Perhaps I am biased, but I believe that in-person events are the most important thing we can do!

The evolution of events shows that while in-person attendance is the medium, events themselves are the tool that brings people together. It's not just about massive parties or large-scale spectacles like the Olympic Games or European soccer tournaments. An event can be any gathering where people unite to share a passion—whether for work, personal growth, or family connections. In these moments, people come together to envision and co-create the future. Events take place in the present, but they help us glimpse what's to come. An incredible example is the Super Bowl, which combines an electrifying in-person atmosphere with millions tuning in worldwide.

Events Are Always in the Present

Events, like life, exist in the present and only in the present. When an event is over and in the past, it becomes a historical fact. It becomes a single line of text in a newspaper article or a Wikipedia page. It becomes a Facebook photo album and a crossed-out section of the calendar. After it is over, the event is no longer alive. It becomes a fixed thing. Once it is over, there is no possibility of new creation or new experiences. The book is closed, and the story is written.

This is why I preach the gospel of events and encourage everyone I meet to go attend events on the subjects they are passionate about. It's like when someone tells you what they think is a funny story, but you don't find it so amusing. The person might say, "You had to be there to get it." Just the same way. You have to be there.

While people at events might discuss the past, they are rooted in the present. Their connection and presence together are about co-creating the future. Even if they don't consciously aim to, they cannot help but move forward. By mapping the power of collective human gatherings, we can harness this to shape the future. In-person is the medium. Without this medium, nothing happens, and everything happens within the container of the present.

When people gather in person, an entire constellation of things happens. There is the energy of the crowd, the excitement of being part of something bigger than oneself, and the serendipitous encounters that can lead to unexpected opportunities. These elements combine to create a powerful, transformative experience that cannot be replicated. This has been the case throughout the thousands or even millions of years of our past evolution, and I firmly believe it will always be the case in our far future.

Because of technology and advancements like AI, the in-person element becomes even more important. It's not just about connecting humans; it's about the myriad of things that happen when we gather together. It's a constellation of experiences that happen in person.

Events are not just gatherings; they are a testament to our innate desire to connect, share, and innovate. When people come together, magic happens. Ideas are exchanged, relationships are forged, and the future is co-created. This alchemy is at the heart of every successful event, driving humanity forward in ways that are both profound and measurable.

If you love motorsport, you probably know that a Formula 1 Grand Prix is thrilling to watch at home or in a venue equipped with screens and race updates. But from the very beginning, these events have been about more than just the action on the track—they're about the collective experience of fans gathering at the circuits. Nothing compares to the atmosphere of being at a Formula 1 race in person; it's an experience that words can't fully capture. And if the local team wins, like Ferrari at the Monza Circuit in Italy, the celebration by the "Tifosi" (Ferrari fans) transforms the event into something truly extraordinary, unforgettable, and beyond belief—an experience that can only be fully appreciated by being there in the moment.

The unique alchemy that occurs during events is absolutely key to our humanity and our evolution into a better world. This alchemy is a blend of knowledge sharing, networking, and the creation of shared experiences. It's where strangers become collaborators and individual insights are woven into a collective tapestry of progress. Events are the heartbeat of human interaction. They are where ideas collide, where new ventures are born, and where the future is envisioned and built. This blending of minds and hearts propels humanity forward.

The Human Story Behind Every Event

Each person who attends an event brings their own unique story and journey. Everyone has their reasons for being there, their own hopes and dreams, and their own connections and experiences. For many, attending an event is a form of pilgrimage, a quest, or a very important mission. It is a chance to be part of something greater than oneself, to contribute to a collective experience, and to take away something meaningful and transformative.

When I walk inside any event, sometimes I also get emotional. I see it as a sort of dream for the people that participate. They spend their life and there is a moment in which they become the hero of the family, their friends, and everything. It's not just, they just take a flight and go there. No, they are living a dream and they have spent their life for that moment. And thanks to that moment, they come back having grown personally and professionally.

For example, every time I walk around an exhibition, I see all the people that have the little booths where they sell their products. I don't see only the surface level of what appears to the physical eyes where a random person is selling some boring product. I see the family of that entrepreneur who, before he took a flight from India to go to sell his product in Germany, has the wife that says, "Good luck!", because it's his life. The daughters come to him and say, "I'll miss you Dad, have a nice flight."

When this man is coming to the exhibition, it's not just a simple story of him taking a flight, arriving, selling something and going back home. I see a human with all the elements that make up him and his life. And I see that he must sell those things, or do whatever he is doing at the exhibition, because it's his life.If he's not able to succeed and he come back home, he will have problems. Maybe he's not able to pay for his girls' school fees or to take his family on a special vacation.

When I walk the floors of a conference or exhibition, no matter how large or small an event it is, I see individual humans who each have their own unique backstory and who are putting everything they can into this event.

When I'm sitting in the audience and a person comes up onto the stage, that guy is presenting years of his knowledge and skills. Maybe he is a doctor and has worked for thousands of hours on something related to a specific disease. When he goes to the stage to speak, maybe he's not even a good speaker, but because he's there in that moment, in that event, in front of other people - he's able to shape the world of medicine. And when he finishes his presentation, people will come up to him, not just to shake his hand, but they will also want to understand how they can apply this in their own medical practice and in their own clinic, hospital, or research facility.

When I see people dancing at a concert after waiting hours to see their favorite artist, I feel the emotions they experienced before the concert—the anticipation and excitement leading up to that "ritual" of liberation. Their dream of being there "in person" is the unique essence of that present moment. It's not just about dancing; it's about being part of a collective dream and shared passion.

Consider sports events - from the athletes to their families and communities watching, there is immense power in those moments. Success is not just about winning; it's about being there together and having that experience as one.

Behind every event, there is a seemingly near-infinite amount of personal history and story, unique experiences, connections to loved ones, and an individual's deep desire to be successful in the field of their passion. It is all there underneath the surface. The event is the present moment and every person who is there brings all of their past into that present, in order to co-create the future.

Serendipity & Synchronicity

Events are hotbeds of connections, serendipity, and synchronicity. They are places where chance encounters can lead to significant breakthroughs, where the right person is met at the right time, and where new ideas are sparked by the simple act of coming together. This is the beauty of events—their ability to create moments of fortune and fate that can change the course of careers, industries, lives, and possibly even the course of humanity itself.

At events, incredible moments occur when you meet someone unexpectedly, and that meeting changes everything. It's the magic of serendipity, the unexpected connections that lead to new opportunities and innovations. It has happened to me many times, and I've heard stories from friends and clients as well; things can happen at events that seem to defy change. We may call it a "coincidence". That may be so, but in my experience, events have a way of magnifying and supercharging the occurrence of coincidences.

After all, when we look at the meaning of the word "coincidence," it literally means "co-incidences," or two incidents happening together. When we gather dozens, hundreds, or even thousands of people together and those people are drawn to a certain place and time because of the call of the event's subject matter – we will find that those people share something in common. In that dynamic soup of swirling energy, there are bound to be incredible instances of serendipity.

It is very important to understand that it is the central nexus point of an event, whether it be an expo, an exhibition, a conference, a sports event, a music festival, or any other form of gathering where these things happen. We may experience serendipity and auspicious chance happenings any day of our lives, but there is something profoundly inexplicable about how an event or gathering seems to create the circumstance and the opportunity for magic to manifest.

The Human Connection

In the past, gathering and connecting in person was absolutely necessary because there were no other possibilities. Events were crucial because they allowed us to meet, exchange ideas, learn, study, and connect. But even then, it wasn't just about physical presence – rather, it was about what could occur through the physical. It was about the energy, the environment, the place, the smells, the noise, the timing, the mood of the people, and so much more.

Countless examples of unique experiences bring people together on a global scale, spanning entertainment, culture, religion, music, and more. Consider Oktoberfest in Munich, Germany—the world's largest entertainment gathering—or Kumbh Mela in India, the most significant religious assembly on the planet. There's Burning Man in Nevada, a massive celebration of art, music, and community, and the Cannes Film Festival in France, which is a pinnacle of the film world. These gatherings are far more than just events; they are extraordinary celebrations of human connection and shared passion.

In-person gatherings are the only type of meeting that can leave a lasting legacy. This legacy remains even after people separate. How many times have you entered a room and smelled something that reminded you of another place and time? There are different layers of legacy. For example, when we organize an event, there's the venue legacy, such as a new stadium that is built. During the event, there's the economic impact on hotels, taxis, restaurants, and tourism. The real legacy is intangible, but it is felt in the internal shift in a person's life, the creation of new innovations, and the shaping of the future.

The true legacy of an event is the transformative impact it has on those who attend. It's the same idea as discussed in part 1 when Kiro met another tribe and exchanged knowledge. It's not just about the immediate connection; it's about the long-term change and innovation that result from these gatherings.

How Events Represent & Crystallize the Present and Create the Future

Events have a unique ability to crystallize the entire past into the present moment, creating a pivotal point that shapes the future. A prime example of this is the Yalta Conference, where the end of World War II was decided.

Held from February 4 to 11, 1945, the Yalta Conference brought together the leaders of the Allied powers: U.S. President Franklin D. Roosevelt, British Prime Minister Winston Churchill, and Soviet Premier Joseph Stalin. They convened in the Livadia Palace near Yalta, Crimea, to discuss the reorganization of post-war Europe and establish a strategy for concluding the war against Germany and Japan. The events of the preceding years, marked by the rise of totalitarian regimes, the failure of appeasement, and the devastation of World War II, culminated in this meeting.

Their discussions crystallized their efforts to establish a framework for lasting peace and reorganization in Europe, setting the stage for the geopolitical landscape of the second half of the 20th century.

However, the conference also set the stage for Cold War tensions, as disagreements over control and influence in Eastern Europe foreshadowed future conflicts between the Western allies and the Soviet Union. The Yalta Conference is often seen as a crucial moment in shaping the post-war world order and the beginning of the geopolitical landscape that defined the second half of the 20th century.

Events like the Yalta Conference highlight how gatherings can represent and crystallize the present, capturing the essence of a moment in time while simultaneously creating a blueprint for the future.

While most of our events aren't exactly as historically impactful as the Yalta Conference, every one is a dynamic confluence where a group of people together co-create the future. We cannot change the past as we are a product of it, but by living in the present and taking action through events and the things that grow out of them, we shape what is to come. This is the foundation of everything. Our future is literally imagined, shaped, chosen, and then enacted through the ritualistic act of gathering together and experiencing what alchemizes in the present moment.

This is the true legacy of events: the continuous chain of human progress driven by the collective experience of gathering together.

The Legacy of Each Event

It's impossible to generalize because each event has so many different variables. But what is important to me is that every event has its own legacy. This legacy can be obvious or more subtle, and it varies greatly depending on the nature of the event.

When we talk about events being a part of human evolution, we must recognize that each event we organize doesn't just end in itself. It opens and expands the possibilities for the next event or phase. Every single event has a legacy, and this legacy can create value for the participants. Whether the event is successful or not, its legacy remains.

Take, for example, large events like Salone del Mobile in Milan, Italy. Milan is famous worldwide as a city of design, fashion, and furniture. My question is: is Milan known as the capital of design and fashion because of the Salone del Mobile, or is the Salone del Mobile in Milan because it is the capital of design and fashion? It is the age-old chicken and the egg conundrum.

The point is that these things reinforce each other. Every year, during Milan's design week, people from all over the world come to Milan. This makes Milan the world's capital of design for one whole week every year. The legacy is that people visit Milan, experience the city, and associate it even more with design. In this way, the event, the city, and the people build this recurring legacy together.

Another crucial element of events is their rituality. Every year, the same things happen in the same place, often with the same people. This creates a long-lasting legacy, which is the main element of events, regardless of their immediate success or failure.

The essence of events lies in their ability to bring people together to see and co-create the future. They are not just about the here and now, but also about the lasting impact on individuals and society. As we move forward, embracing both digital and in-person elements, we must remember the irreplaceable value of physical gatherings. Events are where we connect, innovate, and shape our destiny. They are the heartbeat of human culture and the driving force behind our evolution.

My journey and passion for events underscore the transformative power of these gatherings. Events are where we come together to share our stories, to learn from each other, and to build the future. This is the legacy of events, and I see it as my life's work to continue this tradition and to inspire others to do the same.

CHAPTER 09

Soap Bubbles: The Ephemeral Nature of Events

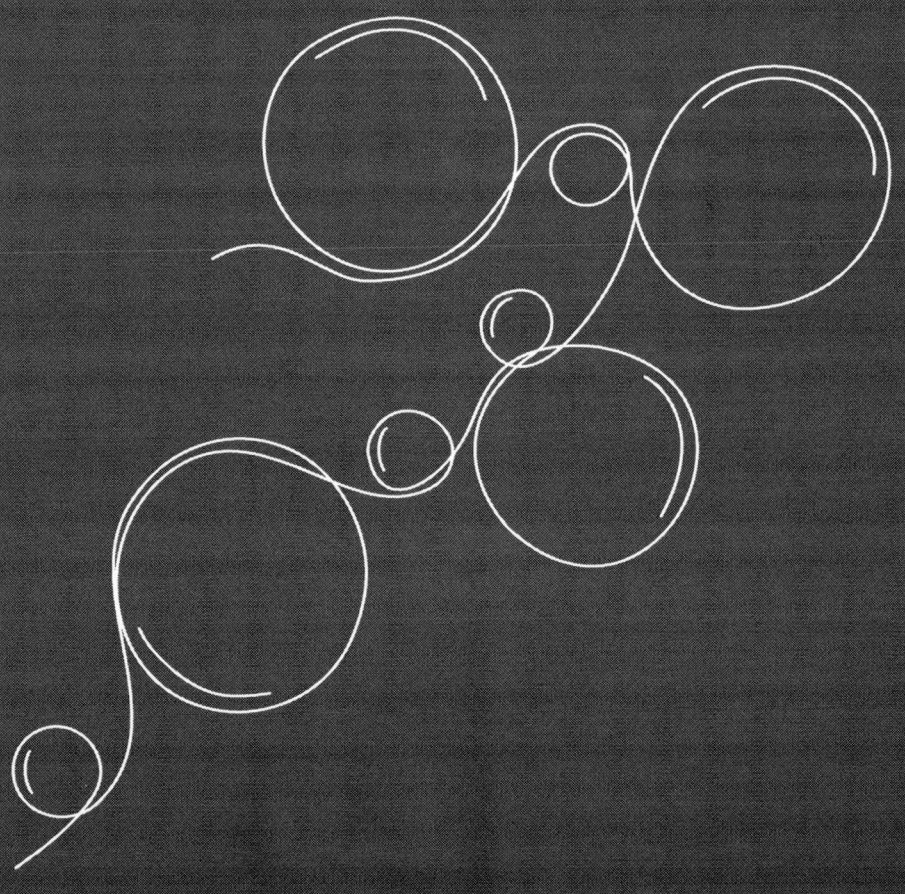

We've all seen children playing with soap bubbles, or perhaps you remember playing with them yourself.

They float through the air in many different sizes and as they do, they catch the light, reflecting a spectrum of colors, drawing the eye with their delicate beauty. Children love to laugh and chase them, they want to grab those bubbles and hold them in their hands, yet they never can. In trying to grasp a bubble it immediately pops. Often children will enjoy the challenge of trying to catch that elusive floating sphere, they will try to catch as many as they can and end that particular temporary bubble of creation. They know full well that there will be many others.

The best metaphor I have found for events is the soap bubble - beautiful and captivating, yet fleeting. They rise, shimmer with vibrant colors, and then disappear, leaving behind a sense of wonder and a trail of memories. The transient nature of events is their magic. They are here one moment and gone the next, a unique and precious confluence of people and circumstances come together just for a few hours or a few days – and then, just as suddenly, the bubble breaks.

For a few moments, there is a shimmer of moisture and color in the air, and then it is gone, leaving no trace of its existence. No trace, except for the lingering effect the conversations and sharings have had on the people, gathered there. For sure, the seeds are planted and will germinate, grow, and finally blossom into new innovations, new connections, and new realities.

Those who attend a truly special event are forever changed. The world they left when they entered the doorway of the event space remains behind, and when they step back out, they enter a new parallel reality. They just spent hours or days immersed in a special place outside of time and space, within a unique bubble, and outside of our normal day-to-day lives. While in this space, their passion has been ignited through coming into contact with others who are expanding the limits of what is possible.

When an event is finished, it is done. Alas, you can't see it anymore and you cannot explain it to another. You either live an event or you don't. There's nothing in between.

The Fleeting Beauty of Events

An event, too, captures our attention and imagination. From the moment the idea is conceived, an event takes on a life of its own. There's a build-up of excitement and anticipation as the date approaches. Every detail is meticulously planned, from the venue and the decorations to the stages and the schedule.

For many industries and niches, there is one main event that occurs on a yearly basis, and it is upon this gathering that their entire business or hobby focuses. This is their annual holy day or sacred week.

Preparations are made months in advance to be prepared to present and engage and put the best foot forward amongst one's peers. Like musicians preparing for a big concert or theater actors preparing for the grand opening performance, there is an energy of nervous excitement and anticipation as the date approaches.

And then, in a burst of energy, the event happens. All the preparations and actions taken only heighten the stakes and the specialness. People gather from around the world, bridging cultures and languages. New connections are made and old ones are forged even stronger as ideas are exchanged back and forth. New memories are created, and perhaps even juicy gossip and drama occurs that leaks out onto social media and to the general public.

Within the container of the venue, an alternate reality is created, and the outside world ceases to matter. For those at the expo or concert/game , everything of interest and importance is occurring right here, right now. And if you are distracted by the outside world, you may miss that moment that sparks the next million-dollar idea, or you may miss making that connection with a new friend, ally, or business partner. While a participant in the event, something deep, archetypal, and primordial is activated within you. You feel deep within you that this communal way of festival, ceremony, and tribal collaboration is essential for a fulfilling and meaningful life as a human being.

The fleeting nature of events intensifies their emotional impact. The anticipation builds as the date approaches, creating a buzz of excitement. When the day finally arrives, the experience is often a whirlwind of sights, sounds, and sensations, leaving participants exhilarated and, at times, overwhelmed. The emotions felt during an event can be profound, creating memories that last a lifetime. This emotional resonance is part of what makes events so special— they leave an indelible mark on our hearts and minds.

But just like the soap bubble, the event soon comes to an end. The decorations are taken down, the venue is emptied, and the participants go their separate ways, carrying with them the echoes of the experience.

And it is good that the event ends, for all special things must remain somewhat rare and unusual. It would not be an event if it did not end, if it happened every day, and if it, therefore, became common and ordinary. No, its value is in its exclusivity. An event is like a moment suspended in time, a brief but powerful burst of human connection and creativity. It's the culmination of countless hours of planning and preparation, brought to life for a fleeting moment.

oOne can rest and reflect after the event. Messages are sent, concrete plans are made, new courses of action are initiated, and the seeds of potentiality and opportunity are given energy to grow. The other 360-odd days of the year are when the actual work is done so that when the next major event cycles around, you have something new to display, to share, to contribute.

Events as Ephemeral Art

I consider events to be a form of ephemeral art. Just as an artist might create a sand mandala, meticulously and painstakingly crafting intricate designs, taking every care to get things absolutely perfect, only to sweep them away once completed. Events too are crafted with care and precision, only to vanish as soon as they occur.

This impermanence gives events a unique intensity and a heightened sense of presence. Participants are aware that they are experiencing something that will never happen in the same way again. It's this impermanence that makes each moment precious, urging attendees to be fully present, to immerse themselves in the experience. The legacy of events is that it is the experience that truly matters and is the heart of it all. Yes, at our gatherings, we may accomplish many practical things, but the most important gift is something intangible and immaterial. It is the experience and how we learn and are changed by it. And, from the effects of that experience within us, everything is changed.

Ephemeral art and events share this incredible power to captivate us with their transience. The knowledge that what we are witnessing is temporary and fleeting makes it all the more beautiful and significant. In a way, this is just like life. If we were immortal and lived forever, we may quickly grow bored. We may wish there was more variety, more surprises, and more uncertainty.

Whether it be a sand painting, an ice sculpture, fireworks, or performance art. These unique works of art are crafted by those who are passionate about them, knowing full well that what they created only lasts as long as it is being created, but as soon as the creation is finished, what they created will already be gone.

The same principle applies to events. The knowledge that an event is temporary adds a layer of urgency and appreciation. Attendees know that they must seize the moment, fully engage, and savor the experience because it will soon be gone – never to be repeated in the same way and with the same people again. Perhaps there will be some videos or pictures that those participating will post online, but these digital simulacra are poor substitutes for the real experience and can never and will never capture the singular magic of being a live participant in that experience of living art. The value expressed during the event is the legacy that will remain and reinforce itself after the end of the live experience.

Recently, I went to a wedding in Greece. As you pass the age of forty, it might be much more difficult to get the chance to attend a wedding of friends. Maybe you more deeply understand the meaning behind a wedding event. It is the moment that the couple truly start a new journey with the deeply significant power of a promise in front of friends and family, in person. The event can be very small, with only a few close friends and family, or it can be large, with hundreds of attendees; however, it is the legacy that will remain for the rest of their lives that is unique.

The Event Blues

While in the midst of the event, one may feel like they are high on a drug. They are meeting so many new and intriguing people, being inspired with new ideas and opportunities, and are in a wondrous new environment such as a foreign country or exciting city. It can feel like the dial of fun and novelty is dialed up to 11.

But what happens when the event is over? After an event, there's often a sense of loss, a feeling of 'What now?' The energy, the connections, the excitement—all of it has dissipated, and you're left with the quiet aftermath.

The "event blues," as I call it, is a common phenomenon, a sense of sadness or emptiness that follows the conclusion of a significant gathering. This feeling arises from the contrast between the intense, shared experience of the event and the return to everyday life.

Managing this emotional transition is crucial for both organizers and attendees. Reflection, sharing memories, and staying connected with fellow participants can help mitigate the post-event letdown, transforming it into a period of appreciation and growth. This is a time for reflection and savoring the memories and integrating the experiences into your life.

Strategies for managing the event blues include creating a post-event ritual, such as sharing photos and stories with other attendees, writing about the experience, or planning a follow-up event. These activities help to keep the spirit of the event alive and provide a sense of closure. For organizers, gathering feedback and reflecting on what worked well and what could be improved can also be a valuable exercise, helping to build on the success of the event and prepare for future endeavors.

A certain amount of come-down is inevitable after a fun and transformative event. My advice would be to allow that passion you experienced to fuel your efforts in your daily life so that you can attend more events and have new gifts to give and experiences to share.

CHAPTER 10

The Event
Life Cycle

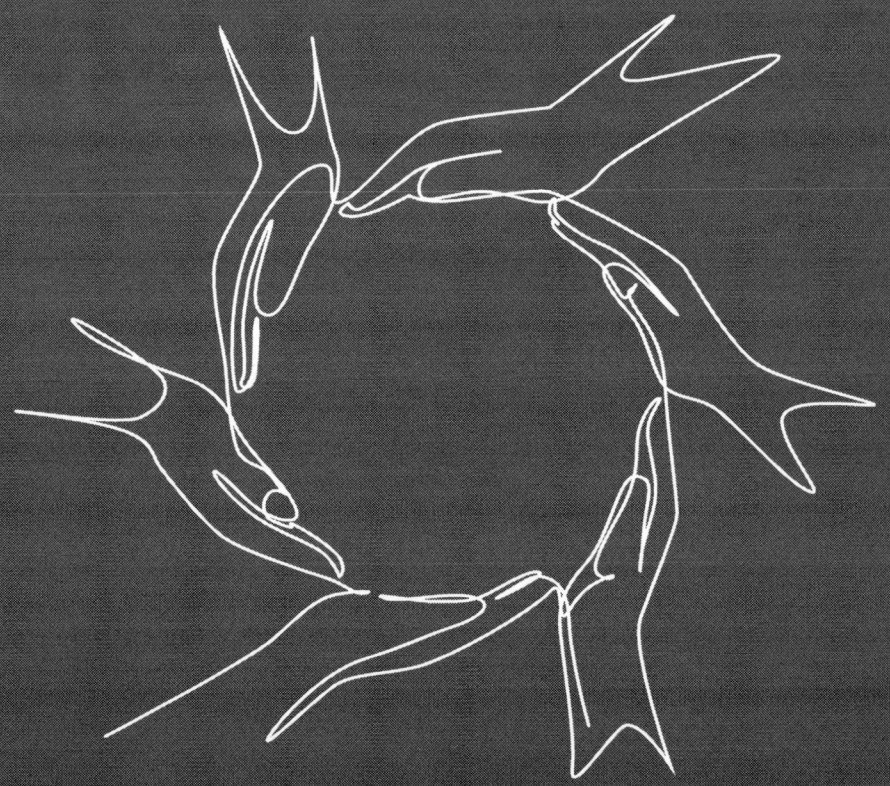

Organizing events is a dynamic and multifaceted endeavor that requires navigating a complex landscape filled with unique challenges and obstacles. This chapter delves into the intricacies of the event industry, exploring the hurdles event organizers face and the innovative solutions they employ to overcome them.

From the seismic impact of the COVID-19 pandemic to personal anecdotes of resilience and success, we will examine case studies that highlight the importance of integrity, passion, and vision.

Through practical insights and strategic methodologies, this chapter aims to equip aspiring event organizers with the tools they need to create impactful and memorable events while also reflecting on the broader implications and long-term benefits of successful event management.

Theory vs. Practice

Understanding the interplay between theory and practice is essential in the realm of event organizing and management. Coming from an academic background with extensive research experience, I've seen firsthand how theory can sometimes seem like a labyrinth of complex numbers and abstract concepts.

However, it's vital to recognize that theory and practice are intrinsically connected. The most effective practices are often grounded in sound theoretical principles.

Think of event management as a microcosm of any professional activity. Mastering the art of organizing events not only equips you with the skills necessary for successful event execution but also enhances your ability to manage various aspects of life. This framework of reasoning and structured approach is invaluable.

By embracing the theory behind event management, we can uncover the best practices that facilitate continuous improvement. It's not just about managing events; it's about adopting a mindset that allows us to improve and excel in our daily endeavors. The key is to consistently apply this framework, turning theoretical knowledge into practical success, and in doing so, significantly enhancing our everyday lives.

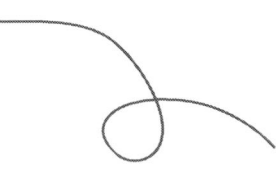

The Event Lifecycle

Understanding the event lifecycle is crucial. It's a central point in event management. To grasp how it works, we use frameworks to follow its process. Though this might seem theoretical, it is highly practical.

The event lifecycle is the backbone of successful event planning and execution. From the initial spark of an idea to the final wrap-up, every stage plays a vital role in creating a memorable experience. It involves a series of interconnected phases, each with its own set of challenges and rewards. By breaking down the lifecycle into manageable segments, we can ensure that no detail is overlooked, and every aspect is optimized for success.

Imagine planning an event as a journey. This journey begins with the inception of an idea, travels through meticulous planning and execution, and culminates in a meaningful conclusion. Understanding each step of this journey is essential for transforming a vision into reality. It allows us to anticipate potential obstacles, allocate resources efficiently, and create events that resonate deeply with attendees. In the following sections, we'll explore the key stages of the event lifecycle, providing insights and strategies to navigate each phase with confidence and creativity.

Understanding the event lifecycle is crucial for anyone involved in event management. It's the backbone that ensures every detail is accounted for and every aspect is optimized for success. Let's delve into the event lifecycle, examining its phases and the dynamics involved in each stage.

The Stages of the Event Lifecycle

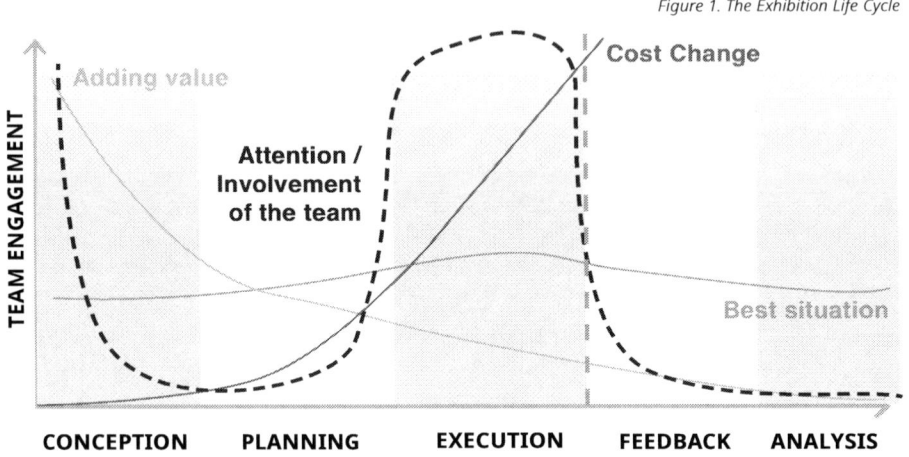

Figure 1. The Exhibition Life Cycle

First, we need to consider two axes. On the Y-axis, we place the team focus(HR Focus), which measures how much the team working on the event is engaged and aligned with the project's goals. This focus is critical to the event's success, whether it's a major event like the Olympic Games or a smaller one like a birthday party. On the X-axis, we place the timeline, which outlines the phases of the event lifecycle.

The first phase is the **Conception Phase.** This is the moment we brainstorm and come up with an idea for the next event. It's the start of all processes, whether for a new event or a new edition of an existing one. During this phase, enthusiasm and creativity are at their peaks, as the team comes together to outline the vision and objectives of the event.

In this phase, I introduce the concept of adding value. This idea is critical to understanding how timing impacts the value of new ideas. In the conception phase, ideas can significantly enhance the event's value. However, as we move closer to the event on the timeline, the potential to add value decreases. This is crucial to remember, as introducing ideas too late in the process can create chaos rather than value.

Often, higher-level team members, such as CEOs or presidents, only engage with the event strategy as the event date approaches. They may feel the pressure and excitement of the impending event and suggest new ideas at the last minute. While these ideas might be great, they can disrupt the established plan and processes.

Following the conception phase is the **Planning Phase**. Planning involves going back and forth to refine and finalize the details of the event. This phase is fundamental because it helps us understand the sequence of activities needed to make the event happen smoothly. It's a time of detailed work, budgeting, scheduling, and logistical planning. Although the excitement may wane during this phase, meticulous planning is what sets the stage for a successful event.

It's vital to integrate new ideas during the conception and planning phases. If a groundbreaking idea emerges late, it's better to consider it for the next event. This approach ensures that the current event runs smoothly and that new ideas can be implemented effectively in future events.

The third phase is the **Execution Phase**, often the most enjoyable for event managers. This is when we put our plans into action. During this phase, the event takes place, and all the preparations come to fruition. The event is now live, marking a critical milestone in the timeline. Energy and focus peak again as the team works together to ensure everything runs smoothly, handling any last-minute issues that arise.

In this stage, we must address the issue of cost changes. The budget for an event tends to remain stable until the last few weeks before the event, after which it can dramatically increase. This surge is due to the costs associated with this phase, which occurs very close to the event date and involves significant uncertainties.

As the event date approaches, the pressure increases, and our ability to make rational decisions decreases. This heightened state of excitement and urgency can lead to inflated costs. For example, booking a projector well in advance might cost a few hundred dollars, but renting one the night before the event can be significantly more expensive.

The same principle applies to other event elements, like decorations. The cost of renting plants for an exhibition booth can skyrocket compared to purchasing them in advance. This discrepancy is due to the urgency and limited options available as the event date nears.

Understanding these cost dynamics helps us prepare better and avoid unnecessary expenses. By planning ahead and making decisions early, we can maintain control over our budget and ensure we're not making rushed, costly choices at the last minute. Keeping these theoretical frameworks in mind allows us to improve our event organization and deliver successful, cost-effective events for our company.

However, the event lifecycle doesn't end with the execution phase. The next crucial stage is the **Feedback Phase**, which occurs during or immediately after the event. Although many people believe the job is done once the event is over, collecting feedback is essential to understand what worked well and what didn't. This phase involves gathering insights from participants, team members, and stakeholders to evaluate the event's success.

The final phase is the **Analysis Phase**. This involves evaluating the feedback to identify areas for improvement. Without proper feedback, the analysis phase cannot be effective. This comprehensive framework helps us continuously improve and align our attitudes and efforts with our goals. It's a reflective period where the team assesses what went well and what could be improved, setting the stage for future events.

Throughout this journey, the team's focus fluctuates. It's highest during the conception phase, where enthusiasm and new ideas are abundant. During the planning phase, focus tends to drop as the work becomes more detailed and less exciting. However, in the execution phase, focus and excitement peak again as the event approaches.

Interestingly, the productivity and energy levels of the team also fluctuate. As the event draws near, adrenaline kicks in, providing a surge of energy and enabling the team to handle numerous tasks efficiently. This high level of activity and stress is akin to the intense experience of childbirth, followed by a period of low energy. I refer to this feeling as the "event blues", and all event organizers experience it and know it very well.

After the event, there is often a noticeable drop in productivity and mood. This "event blues" period is common and affects everyone involved. It's important to recognize this phase and understand that it's part of the process. During this time, gathering feedback might be challenging due to the team's low energy levels, but it is crucial for the analysis phase.

In summary, the event lifecycle includes the conception, planning, execution, feedback, and analysis phases. Understanding and managing each phase effectively ensures continuous improvement and successful event management. By navigating through these phases with a clear framework, event managers can create impactful and memorable experiences that resonate with attendees long after the event has concluded.

Practical Example: A Child's Birthday Party

Let's dive into a practical example to illustrate the concepts of the event lifecycle. Imagine you're organizing an eight-year-old's birthday party. This seemingly simple event can provide a comprehensive look at each phase of the lifecycle.

CONCEPTION PHASE

The idea is to have a grand birthday celebration for your child, so you decide to host a pizza party at your apartment, inviting family, friends, classmates, and their parents. The goal is to create a fun and memorable experience for your daughter and her friends.

PLANNING PHASE

The planning phase begins with setting a date and ensuring it works for most guests. You check with local pizzerias to see if they can deliver 20 pizzas at 8 PM on the chosen day. Additionally, you consult your wife to ensure she agrees with the plan and check if your daughter has any specific requests, such as a unicorn-themed cake. Finding a bakery that can make this special cake becomes a priority.

You also consider logistics: creating a guest list, sending out invitations, and forming a WhatsApp group to coordinate with the guests. Your wife suggests hiring a nanny to manage the children so that adults can relax and enjoy the party. You agree and start looking for a nanny, finalizing details to ensure everything runs smoothly.

EXECUTION PHASE

As the event day approaches, the execution phase kicks in. Despite meticulous planning, unexpected challenges arise. The nanny cancels at the last minute, causing a scramble to find a replacement. You make a quick trip to the grocery store to buy additional supplies, including special unicorn-themed dishes and glasses and some alcoholic beverages for the adults.

On the day of the event, you coordinate the pizza delivery, manage decorations, and ensure the venue is set up perfectly. The children are excited, and the adults are ready to enjoy a relaxed evening. Despite some initial chaos, the party gets underway.

EVENT DAY: LIVE PHASE

The live phase of the event is where everything comes together. The guests arrive, the pizzas are delivered, and the party begins. However, you quickly realize that the pizzeria struggles to manage the large order, resulting in some pizzas arriving cold. You have to improvise and throw a few pizzas in the oven to warm them up.

One child falls from the swing and needs some simple medical care in the form of a band-aid and some nurturing for her tears. However, she quickly bounces back and rejoins the other children who are having a blast with games and activities while the adults enjoy the food and drinks. Despite the hiccup with the pizza and the minor injury, the event is a success, and everyone leaves with smiles on their faces.

FEEDBACK PHASE

Immediately after the party, you gather feedback from the guests. Some mention that the pizza was cold or that it was a bit too hot outside in the sun, which detracted from the experience. This feedback is crucial for understanding what went well and what needs improvement. You take notes and consider what changes could be made for future events.

ANALYSIS PHASE

In the analysis phase, you evaluate the feedback and overall success of the party. You realize that while the event was generally successful, the issue with the cold pizza could have been avoided with better planning. Next time, you might stagger the pizza delivery or choose a pizzeria with a better capacity to handle large orders. The analysis helps you refine your approach and improve future events.

REFLECTION AND CONTINUOUS IMPROVEMENT

Reflecting on this birthday party, you understand that no event is perfect, but each one offers valuable lessons. Blending theory with practice, you develop frameworks that make you stronger and more capable of managing events. Whether it's a large-scale event like the Olympics or an everyday gathering like a child's birthday party, each event contributes to enhancing your overall quality of life.

As you can see from this simple everyday example, mastering the event lifecycle—from conception and planning to execution, feedback, and analysis—ensures continuous improvement and successful event management. Our lives are a series of events, and improving how we manage them enhances our overall quality of life.

Feedback and Analysis

Since the feedback and analysis phases of the event life cycle are so critical and pivotal for continuous improvement, there are a few more things I'd like to share with you.

To review, **Feedback** is the valuable information we collect from our clients, suppliers, team members, and all other stakeholders (governments, opinion leaders, friends, etc.). It encompasses all insights that can create value for future events. Feedback is crucial because it provides explicit insights from everyone involved in our event. Without it, we risk repeating the same mistakes and missing opportunities for enhancement.

Analysis involves a thorough review of the entire event life cycle. This phase is about understanding what we did, using all the feedback collected, and integrating these insights into our strategy. The goal is continuous improvement. It's not just about how to do things but understanding why we do them. The framework we use focuses on strategic decision-making. Listening is fundamental in event management. This means systematically collecting and connecting information—not random comments from unreliable sources, but data that forms the basis for strategic decisions.

Event management is complex, but by collecting information within a specific framework and using Key Performance Indicators (KPIs), we can develop effective strategies. Investing as much time in analysis as we do in planning, construction, and execution will lead to significant improvements and better future events.

Focus on Experience

I always emphasize the importance of customer experience. Cost is often seen as a complex issue, but any cost in a company can be reduced. Costs include everything from utilities and office rentals to personnel and marketing expenses. Reducing costs is straightforward, but focusing solely on cost-cutting is not sustainable.

Revenues are the real focus, and they come from customers. Customer satisfaction is crucial for achieving customer loyalty, which is the only way to secure future revenues. In the event industry, finding new customers is much more difficult and expensive than retaining existing ones.

Satisfied customers create a community that adds value to our events. A loyal customer is part of this community and can help attract other enthusiastic customers. This community grows as we satisfy our clients, suppliers, and stakeholders. Loyal customers trust our company, allowing us to offer additional products and services beyond just event-related offerings. This includes cross-selling, suggesting products, and guiding them to other events or activities provided by our company.

What is Satisfaction?

The concept of satisfaction is fundamental to those who wish to organize and host successful events. Satisfaction can be understood through a simple equation: **Satisfaction = Experience/**Expectation. This means that satisfaction is determined by the relationship between experience and expectation.

Let's consider a relatable example: I'm Italian and living in Dubai. Suppose someone asks me to recommend the best Italian restaurant in Dubai, and I suggest Luigia at the Rixos Hotel. The person trusts my opinion, so their expectation for Luigia rises significantly. They go to Luigia with high expectations, but if the experience is less than perfect (e.g., a mistake in their order), their satisfaction decreases, even if the food is good. This demonstrates that higher expectations make it harder to achieve satisfaction.

From an anthropological perspective, humans are wired to spread negative experiences faster than positive ones. This highlights the importance of managing expectations to ensure satisfaction. In the event industry, we often create unrealistic expectations by claiming each event is the "best edition ever" or "the only place to be." When reality falls short, it leads to dissatisfaction and lower loyalty.

Managing expectations is crucial. It's not about downplaying the event but being honest and realistic. This way, the actual experience can meet or exceed expectations, leading to higher satisfaction and loyalty. As you can see, blending theory with practice allows us to develop frameworks that make us stronger and more capable of managing events, from large-scale ones like the Olympics to everyday gatherings.

The Attention Spike

The power of an event lies in its ability to create a significant spike of attention before, during, and immediately after it takes place. This spike is not just for the organizer, but for everyone involved. Attendees focus intensely on that niche, that specific event, and that particular moment in time. For example, in the wine industry, the month of April, when the major wine fair occurs, becomes a focal point. All attention, connections, and energy are concentrated on this event. The rest of the year involves maintaining relationships with suppliers and customers, but it is this intense period of focus that defines the rituality of the event.

Rituality, by nature, must be periodic. You cannot have a ritual every day; that would simply become ordinary life. The spike of attention created by an event is a manifestation of this rituality. It's essential to understand that while maintaining engagement is important, the extraordinary nature of the event itself cannot be replicated continuously. The major event creates a peak experience, a "wow" moment that stands out.

Throughout the year, there can be smaller spikes—conferences, webinars, newsletters, mini-tours, and conventions—that help maintain connection and engagement within the community. These activities support the main event, but they do not replace the unique impact of the big moment.

Many in the event industry argue for constant high engagement, suggesting that events should be continuous, lasting 365 days a year. I strongly disagree.

Such an approach dilutes the very essence of what makes events special. The event is the culmination of planning, anticipation, and energy, creating a powerful and memorable experience that cannot be sustained indefinitely. A constantly high level of engagement would make the event less significant, turning it into an ordinary routine rather than an extraordinary experience.

It is crucial to have tools and platforms that keep the community connected and engaged throughout the year. These can serve as repositories of content, networking opportunities, and other resources. However, expecting the same level of intensity every day undermines the unique power of the event itself. The ritualistic spike of attention before, during, and after the event is what makes it impactful and memorable.

THE FUTURE
OF EVENTS

PART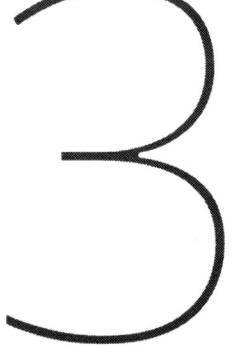

CHAPTER 11

Events Today:
The Digital Shift

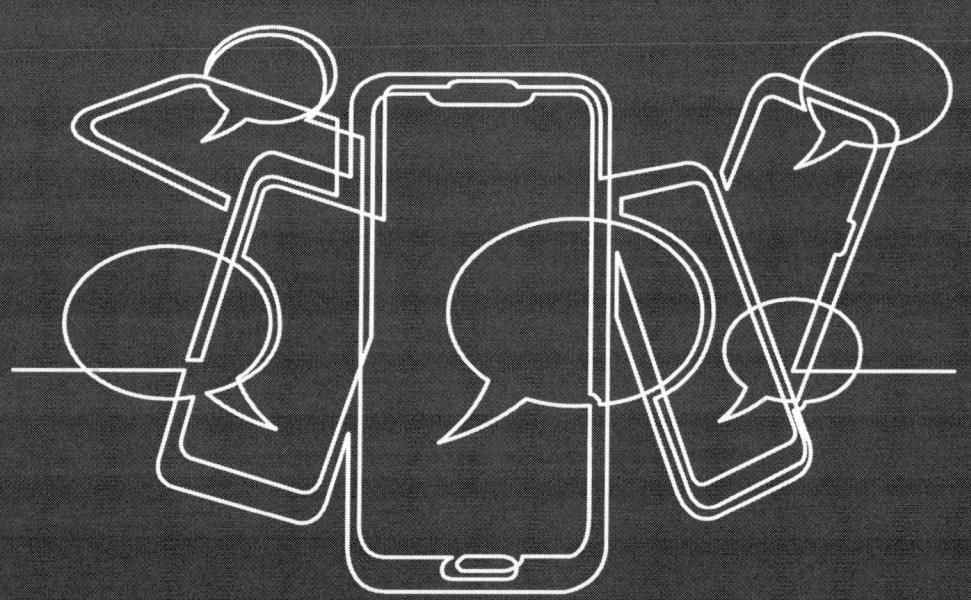

The nature of modern events is undergoing a profound transformation, driven by the relentless pace of technological advancement. This era, marked by the digital shift, is not just a phase in the evolution of events it's a complete re-imagining of how we connect, share, and experience gatherings. The digital revolution, with its high-speed internet and cutting-edge technologies, has dramatically altered the way we think about and execute events.

The rapid adoption of digital tools was significantly accelerated by the COVID-19 pandemic, which necessitated a swift transition to virtual gatherings. Zoom web conferencing and other digital platforms became essential, allowing people to connect and hold events from the safety of their homes. This shift highlighted both the potential and the limitations of digital events. While it offered a temporary solution, it also underscored the irreplaceable value of real, physical, in-person gatherings.

In this chapter, we will explore the various facets of this digital transformation. We will examine how COVID-19 acted as a catalyst for the digitalization of events and discuss the integration of technology in modern event planning. We will delve into the concept of "phygital" experiences, which blend physical and digital elements to create immersive and engaging interactions. Additionally, we will look at how digital tools have redefined the way we interact during events and how they ensure continuity and engagement after the event has concluded. Finally, we will consider the role of global event brands in a localized context and how technology is bridging the gap between global reach and local relevance.

I hope to provide a comprehensive understanding of how the digital shift is reshaping the event industry. By examining both the opportunities and challenges that come with this transformation, we can better appreciate the enduring importance of in-person gatherings while embracing the innovative potential of digital technologies. The digital era has opened up new possibilities for the event industry, but it has also reinforced the timeless value of human connection and the unique magic of physical events.

Navigating the Event Industry During COVID-19

Our industry has tried its best to forget COVID, but some memories are hard to erase. During that time, I was being interviewed and they asked me, "How do you sleep as an entrepreneur in the event industry during COVID?" I thought for a moment and then replied, "I sleep like a baby."

The interviewer looked puzzled and asked, "Why?"

I said, "Because I wake up six or seven times a night screaming and asking for my mother!"

That pretty much sums up the period. It was a disaster. However, I think many good things have come from that event and it has taught us much about the nature and importance of events. I think it can also teach us how to navigate worldwide crisis events that may happen in the future.

In August 2019, my company won the tender for Expo 2020 Dubai. Everything was booming, and things were looking great for the future. At the beginning of 2020, to celebrate my wife's 40th birthday, we traveled to the Maldives and stayed in five-star hotels. It was a dream come true, but as we returned to Dubai, the world was starting to hear whispers about COVID-19. Suddenly, in less than three weeks, our future business looked uncertain, and we calculated that we could potentially lose up to 93% of our revenue that year.

Despite the grim outlook, my wife and I decided to invest all our savings into the company. With the support of our business partner and the entire team, we decided to do everything possible to survive. I had an unshakeable belief that events would come back stronger than ever. This social distancing, I believed, would only deepen our understanding of the importance of human gatherings.

And I was right.

When COVID-19 hit, our entire event industry was in turmoil. My company was expecting to be busy with all our usual big events to organize, plus the very large and important Expo 2020 Dubai project, but everything just stopped, including Expo 2020 Dubai, which was postponed for a year. Instead of opening in October 2020, the Global Expo was rescheduled for October 2021, giving us a year to survive. Despite cutting costs across the board, Expo 2020 Dubai retained us to develop new customer experiences tailored to the pandemic era. This decision was a lifeline.

During this challenging period, the Dubai government also reached out to us. In April 2020, amid the global lockdown, they wanted to launch an event in June 2020 and needed our help. They wanted us to gather data on safety measures, get insight on visitor, sponsor, and exhibitor perspectives, as well as thoughts and ideas that would allow the event industry to restart.

We compiled all possible data from every possible touchpoint showing that, with high safety standards, people were still willing to attend events, provided some specific "distance" factors that then became a global standard were implemented. The first event in June was an incredibly successful experiment, and we collected a ton of insights, suggestions and points of view from the many beneficiaries of the event, including visitors, sponsors, opinion leaders, governments, exhibitors, and more. By September 2020, using our data, Dubai's Ministry of Tourism officially announced the reopening of the city's events industry, and by December 2020, they held the 2020 Gitex Global event, also based on our recommendations.

It was a tough couple of years, but I am proud that my company did not let anyone go. We spent every penny we had and took loans, fully believing the industry would bounce back. Our faith paid off. While many companies were trying to exit from the event industry, we had the opportunity to acquire one of the most important event registration companies, named Info Salon. Even if the period was not the right one to invest in the live in-person event industry, my personal passion and belief in the power of events was the driver to finalize the purchase during the turbulent COVID time.

Despite the chaos, we were positioned uniquely. The industry was in a lull, but thanks to the Expo 2020 Dubai Project we were able to keep ourselves afloat and even grow during this period. This time highlighted how, even amidst a crisis, opportunities can arise if you're prepared and willing to take risks. I already mentioned that I feel that I am a very lucky person, and it seems to be so!

The Legacy of COVID-19

COVID-19 changed the landscape of event organizing fundamentally. Travel became difficult and expensive, but the demand for in-person events remained strong. The quality of attendees improved significantly, with more CEOs and top executives attending events instead of mid-level managers. The silver lining of COVID-19 is that experiencing a time of social isolation underscored the importance of face-to-face interactions, which virtual meetings simply cannot replicate.

Today, the event industry is booming, and events worldwide are much bigger, stronger, and more important than ever. Thanks to COVID-19 and the lockdowns that governments worldwide mandated, we now perfectly understand the importance of in-person meetings. Yes, on a daily or weekly basis it is fine to talk through Zoom or FaceTime, but at least once or twice per year, we need to have the ritualistic event where we meet , with the unique constellation of things that only in face-to-face interactions can happen.

Zoom and other online platforms may have been able to act as a substitute for some classes, conferences, university lectures, and council meetings, but large events, concerts, and exhibitions are different. They require an in-person presence to fully appreciate and engage with the vibe, the overall atmosphere and fun, or the products and innovations on display. No matter how much our technology evolves, it can never replace the in-person human experience.

To give just one example, a unique immersive experience like a music festival or the complex purchase of industrial machinery cannot be adequately conducted through a screen. From one side, the tribe meeting creates an almost "spiritual" relief for the participant. On the other hand, the "business side", the seller and the buyer must be able to look at the product, touch it, and see it in action with their own eyes while comparing and being immersed in a vast exhibition focused within their niche.

Large concerts are nice to watch on YouTube from your couch, but the feeling and overall physical experience is much more immersive than any video could ever be. This is why I preach the gospel of live, in-person events! They provide a unique opportunity for hands-on interaction, intimate communion, and networking that mediated digital and virtual platforms cannot match.

COVID-19 was a wake-up call. It reinforced the value of in-person gatherings and the unique experiences they offer. The pandemic forced the events industry itself to innovate and adapt, but it also highlighted the irreplaceable nature of physical events. Today, the event industry is more mature and able to interact and integrate many technologies to boost the in-person experience, with higher attendance and greater engagement than ever before. So, rather than destroy the live event industry, the COVID-19 event revitalized it and breathed new life into those who attend.

The crisis taught us resilience and the importance of adapting quickly to new circumstances. For anyone facing a similar crisis, the key is to stay calm, invest in your core strengths, and be ready to seize new opportunities. The future is uncertain, but with strong values, the right mindset, and proper strategies, it is possible to navigate through the toughest challenges and come out stronger.

The lessons from COVID-19 are clear: adaptability, resilience, and a strong belief in the value of human connection are essential. As we move forward, it's important to remember the importance of in-person interactions. No matter how advanced our technology becomes, nothing can replace the unique magic of being physically present with others. For those in the event industry, staying ahead means continuously learning, adapting, and believing in the transformative power of events.

The Integration of Technology in Modern Events

The integration of technology into modern events has been nothing short of revolutionary. From the moment of conceptualization to the event's culmination, technology plays a pivotal role, augmenting and facilitating the entire event experience.

Advanced registration systems enable a more streamlined, personalized approach to attendee management, ensuring that each participant's experience is tailored and meaningful. These systems go beyond simple ticketing, offering features like pre-event surveys and personalized agendas that enhance the overall experience for attendees.

Matchmaking algorithms employed by event platforms have redefined networking, connecting visitors and sponsors or exhibitors with unparalleled precision in a way that allows everyone to leverage the "live" experience. This digital facilitation extends beyond mere introductions, fostering meaningful business relationships and collaborations. Attendees can now effortlessly connect with the right people, ensuring that each interaction is purposeful and valuable.

RFID technology and smart badges have revolutionized the way we track and manage attendee movements within events. These technologies provide real-time data on attendee behavior, helping organizers understand flow patterns, popular sessions, and networking hotspots. This data-driven approach enables more effective event planning and improved attendee experiences.

Virtual and augmented reality are also making significant inroads into the event space. These technologies offer immersive experiences that were previously unimaginable. Virtual reality can transport attendees to different locations or provide interactive product demonstrations, while augmented reality can enhance on-site experiences with interactive exhibits and real-time information overlays.

Incorporating live streaming and on-demand content has expanded the reach of events beyond physical boundaries. Attendees who cannot be physically present can still participate in sessions, engage with speakers, and network with other attendees. This hybrid model ensures inclusivity and maximizes the event's impact.

Mobile apps have become indispensable tools for modern events, offering features like real-time updates, interactive maps, and personalized schedules. These apps enhance attendee engagement by providing a centralized platform for information and interaction. Many b2b organizers are now utilizing a blending of tech and human experience and the niche of exhibitions is moving more and more in this direction, as evidenced by large multinationals like the (RX) Reed Exhibition and Informa Markets.

However, it is essential to recognize that while technology enhances the logistics and efficiency of events, the essence of gatherings remains the human connection and the shared experience. Technology should be seen as a tool to amplify these connections rather than replace them. The spiritual and emotional aspects of being physically present at an event cannot be fully replicated by digital means. Amidst all these advancements, the true power of events lies in the human connections they foster and the shared moments they create. Technology should enhance these experiences, making them more accessible, efficient, and engaging while preserving the irreplaceable magic of in-person gatherings.

Phygital Experiences

The concept of the phygital experience—blending physical and digital elements—has become increasingly relevant in modern events. While digital experiences provide support and convenience, they are not a complete substitute for physical presence.

Today, we recognize the hyper-segmentation of needs and experiences. In events, a mobile app might be highly useful for some attendees, providing schedules, networking opportunities, and real-time updates. Yet, for others, it might hold little value as they prioritize direct, personal interactions and only the pure physical presence.

The phygital approach acknowledges that different attendees have varying needs and preferences. Technology can significantly enhance the event for some, offering tools for networking, navigation, and engagement. However, it is not a one-size-fits-all solution. The core experience of being physically present at an event, engaging directly with others, and immersing oneself in the environment, remains irreplaceable.

Moreover, the post-event engagement and community-building facilitated by digital tools are critical. This trend has been a focal point in the event industry for years, highlighting the importance of maintaining connections and engagement long after the event concludes. Digital platforms can help sustain the community, offering forums, follow-up content, and networking opportunities that extend the event's impact.

This is why I believe that while digital elements can significantly enhance an event, they should only serve as supplementary tools rather than replacements. The true essence of an event lies in the physical gathering of people, where personal interactions and shared experiences create lasting memories. However, the phygital approach can strike a balance, leveraging technology to enhance the event while preserving the irreplaceable value of in-person engagement.

Registration & Ticketing:
The Beating Heart of Data in Events

Before the event, technology plays a crucial role in setting the stage for a successful gathering. Registration is the core of the "data" and the beginning of the visitor experience, but not the only thing. The process has become highly streamlined and very customizable for every event niche through specific and highly advanced companies that serve the event industry and are highly specialized in this field,

In the vast and intricate ecosystem of events, where technology has permeated every aspect of organization and management, the registration process emerges as a crucial element, often underestimated, but fundamentally important. Registration is not just the beginning of the visitor's journey; it represents the pivotal point where the digital and physical worlds converge, creating an experience that is as technological as it is human.

Registration is much more than a simple technical step to gain entry to an event. It is the moment when data becomes people, and people transform into participants. This simple-appearing process is a sophisticated art. It is an operation that requires precision, expertise, and a deep understanding of the events sector, the local market's needs, and all the complexities of human interactions at a venue before entering the event.

Imagine a visitor sitting at their computer, entering their details to register for a concert, an exhibition, trade show, or conference. At that moment, their identity begins to be digitized, transformed into a series of information that the organizer must manage with utmost care.

The real task of the organizer, however, is not just to collect and safeguard this data but to also ensure that the person who attends the event is indeed the one who registered. This demands perfect integration between online and offline components, between the digital world and the in-person experience, creating a symphony of operations that culminates in physical access to the event.

Many people might consider registration as a given, almost automatic. However, nothing could be further from the truth. Registration is a complex IT process where security, accuracy, and flexibility are essential elements. It's not just about allowing a person to enter an event, but also about ensuring that the data collected is authentic, verified, and usable in every subsequent phase of the participant's experience.

The process doesn't end with the online submission of data; that's merely the beginning. When the visitor arrives at the event, the data must be reconverted into a person, and this must happen smoothly, quickly, and without errors. It is at this moment that the registration process reveals its true complexity, as it must function perfectly despite the variables that every event entails, from the different nature of events to regional peculiarities.

It is precisely this complexity that has seen technology giants like Amazon and Microsoft fail in their attempts to dominate this field. Event registration requires a level of expertise and understanding that goes beyond pure technology; it demands a deep knowledge of the dynamics of live events, the expectations of participants, and the cultural nuances.

Another crucial aspect of registration is often overlooked: its function as a marketing tool. The registration process is not just a bureaucratic formality but also a critical moment where the organizer has the opportunity to communicate with the participant, to prepare them for the experience that awaits them, and to build their expectations. In a world where the onsite experience is as important as the online one, registration represents the first real contact between the event and its audience.

Oversimplifying this process, making it akin to a trivial online purchase, risks trivializing the importance of physical participation in an event. Registration is, in fact, a moment of learning, of preparation, where the participant begins to build their agenda, understand the value of the event, and align with what lies ahead. Removing or diminishing the importance of this process means losing a valuable opportunity to establish a deep connection with the visitor.

Event organizers must understand the importance of relying on experts to manage the complexity of the ticketing and registration process. This is not just a strategic choice but an operational necessity. Developing the technologies needed for an effective registration process internally requires enormous investments, not only in the initial development phase but especially in maintaining and continually evolving these technologies, which must remain at the forefront to meet the standards of security, flexibility, and interoperability required by modern events, through all the various devices.

The mistake of underestimating this process can lead to severe consequences, not only in terms of event management but also in terms of visitor experience, data security, and the ability to meet the diverse needs of an increasingly demanding and varied audience.

The registration process is not just a necessary step to participate in an event; it is also the fulcrum around which the entire data ecosystem powering the in-person experience revolves. It is an art that requires mastery, knowledge, and a clear vision of the data's crucial role in creating memorable and safe events.

Only through conscious and expert management of this process can organizers ensure that the visitor's experience is seamless, secure, and, most importantly, authentic. Registration is ultimately the starting point of an extraordinary journey that transforms data into people and people into active participants in a collectively co-created future through the event experience.

Advanced algorithms can manage attendee lists, send reminders, and even offer demand-based dynamic pricing. The most advanced ticketing providers are able to create hyper-segmented visitor's experiences.

Promoting the event has also evolved with digital tools. Event organizers can leverage social media, email marketing, and online advertising to generate pre-event buzz and hype. These platforms enable targeted campaigns that reach the right audience, creating anticipation and excitement. Social media platforms, in particular, allow potential attendees to connect, share their expectations, and build a community even before the event begins. Influencers and brand ambassadors can further amplify the event's reach, engaging their followers and driving interest.

Pre-Event Promotion: Targeted Strategies to Engage and Prepare Attendees

Promoting an event today requires a well-defined strategy that distinguishes between two key groups: those who have yet to register and those who have already completed their registration. This differentiation is crucial to maximize the effectiveness of pre-event communication and ensure that every participant arrives well-prepared and motivated.

For those who haven't registered yet, the promotional strategy should focus on creating a sense of urgency and highlighting the importance of early registration. Utilizing marketing techniques such as limited-time offers, exclusive benefits for early sign-ups, or emphasizing the advantages of being among the first to register can encourage potential attendees to take that initial step.

The goal is to prevent the registration process from being postponed, as early registration allows participants to better prepare, plan their schedule, and approach the event with greater awareness.

On the other hand, for those who have already registered, it's essential to implement a communication strategy that provides useful and crucial information to maximize their event experience. This can include details on how to navigate the event, information about the sponsors and the exhibitors, session schedules, and even tips on how to connect with other attendees.

The idea is to guide the participant through a preparation journey that ensures they are ready to make the most of their time at the event.

However, it's important to acknowledge that, particularly in B2B events, attendees often tend to register at the last minute, creating a significant challenge for organizers. This makes it even more important to have a promotional strategy that keeps interest and engagement high throughout the pre-event period, ensuring that even last-minute registrants receive all the necessary information to have a successful experience.

A well-orchestrated promotion must balance the push for early registration with adequate preparation for those already registered, ensuring that every individual arrives at the event equipped with all the resources they need for a complete and rewarding experience.

During the Event:
A New Digital Interaction Paradigm

As the event unfolds, the interaction with attendees enters a more sophisticated phase, where the physical presence of the participant must be seamlessly integrated with digital engagement through their mobile devices. In this stage, event apps and live websites become indispensable tools, serving as the central hub for real-time information, interaction, and personalized experiences.

The efforts made during the pre-event phase lay the groundwork for what happens once the event is live. The information shared beforehand becomes crucial for arriving, accessing, and navigating the event, but the interaction needs to evolve to meet the real-time needs of the attendees. These needs vary significantly depending on the type of event.

For instance, at a concert, the most valuable information may revolve around the venue logistics, while at a B2B event, the focus shifts to the content, including conference sessions, networking opportunities, and, most importantly, the exhibitors' stands or sponsors. These are the very reasons participants choose to travel and attend in person.

The event itself has transformed into a rich digital landscape, creating a new interaction paradigm. Tools like lead scanning and real-time data collection have become standard, allowing exhibitors to capture and analyze attendee interactions efficiently. This technology enables immediate follow-ups and personalized engagement, significantly enhancing the overall experience for both attendees and exhibitors.

Digital platforms facilitate continuous interaction among all parties, effectively breaking down the barriers of time and space. Attendees can use event apps to navigate the venue, access schedules, participate in live polls, or engage in Q&A sessions. These technological advancements have given rise to 'phygital' experiences—a blend of physical and digital realities that enrich the attendee experience. Technologies such as Augmented Reality (AR), Virtual Reality (VR), and interactive displays have become commonplace, turning events into immersive, multi-sensory experiences. Participants can explore virtual exhibits, interact with digital avatars, and engage with content in ways that were previously unimaginable.

In this dynamic environment, the role of digital tools is not just to complement the physical experience but to elevate it, providing attendees with a more engaging, personalized, and memorable event. As a result, the distinction between the physical and digital aspects of the event blurs, creating a cohesive, integrated experience that meets the diverse needs and expectations of today's event-goers.

After the Event:
Continuity and Engagement

**The end of the physical event is no longer the end of the expe-
rience. Instead, it marks the beginning of a new phase crucial
for building a bridge and a lasting relationship with participants for the future. While digital platforms offer the possibility of
maintaining continuous interaction under the event brand, it
is essential to understand that an in-person event remains the
core of the entire experience.**

The idea of keeping a digital event active 365 days a year is
inherently flawed because it no longer represents an event
but rather a continuous interaction platform. What is truly
important is to envision a post-event interaction system
composed of multiple variables and moments for building
relationships with the visitor.

In this context, the role of post-event feedback becomes
essential. During and after the event, it is crucial to open a
dialogue with the participant—not only to gather valuable
data to improve future events but also to establish a relationship based on the understanding that the organizer's
role is to optimize and enhance the next experience. Therefore, participant feedback is not just a collection of opinions but an added value that becomes an integral part of
their experience.

Post-event engagement strategies include sharing recor-
ded sessions, providing access to event highlights, and
creating discussion forums where attendees can continue
networking and exchanging ideas. This perpetual engagement ensures that the momentum generated by the event
is not lost but rather built upon. This leads to ongoing community building and knowledge sharing, transforming a single event into a long-term relationship.

Organizers can also gather feedback through surveys and
analytics, using this data to improve future events. By maintaining a vibrant and active online presence, events can re-

main relevant and continue to provide value to their communities long after the last attendee has left the venue.

In essence, technology has revolutionized the way we plan, execute, and follow up on events. It has created new opportunities for engagement and interaction, making events more dynamic and impactful. By integrating digital tools before, during, and after the event, organizers can enhance the attendee experience, foster lasting connections, and ensure the event's success and longevity.

The Strategic Value of Data in Events: From Collection to Analysis

In the increasingly complex and sophisticated world of events, data represents the true strategic asset for organizers. The collection of data during the pre-event, the event itself, and the post-event phases creates an invaluable information resource.

However, the real potential of this data lies not just in its collection but in the ability to analyze it, study it, and transform it into actionable knowledge that can guide future strategic decisions.

Event organizers must understand the importance of data, especially when it's thoroughly analyzed. While event organization is by nature a more operational and managerial activity, data analysis belongs to the realm of research companies, which possess the necessary skills and tools to transform raw data into valuable insights.

One of the key aspects to understand is that data analysis, study, and deep examination must necessarily be entrusted to external experts. The role of an external research company is crucial because it offers a "detached" perspective, acting as a critical filter that allows for a more objective and comprehensive understanding. This is essential because the organizer is inherently deeply involved in the dynamics of the event and cannot also serve as an impartial observer. To have a clear and unbiased view, the observer and the subject of observation must remain distinct.

At a mature stage of development, an event organizer must recognize their own limitations and acknowledge the added value of turning to experts in data research and analysis. These specialists can maximize the real return for the organizer, providing a deeper and more strategic understanding of the event's dynamics.

The role of a research company is not to provide ready-made answers but to offer methods and tools to understand the best way to stimulate strategic questions. This element is fundamental: a good research company is not just a data provider but a strategic partner that helps the organizer navigate the complexities of events.

This is why it is essential to work with research companies specializing in the niche of events, particularly "live" events. Events are an extremely sophisticated industry with many nuances, and only a research company with specific experience and expertise can fully understand the dynamics and depth required to manage and create valuable insights from the collected data.

This activity cannot and should not be carried out by the organizers themselves. This is not only to avoid a natural "bias"—given the emotional and operational involvement of the organizer—but also because the organizer does not possess the necessary skills, tools, and, most importantly, the method required for effective data analysis. The value of data lies not simply in having it but in the ability to make it usable, useful, and strategically relevant for the owner.

Today, event organizers must understand that the true potential of the data collected during all phases of an event can only be realized through thorough analysis conducted by external and specialized experts. This approach not only enhances the value of the data but also transforms it into a powerful tool for continuously improving the participant experience and ensuring the long-term success of the event. We will have a deeper and more advanced dissertation on the importance of data in the next chapter: Chapter 12: The Ascendency of Data.

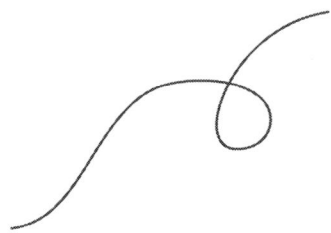

Global Event Brands and Localization

In the dynamic landscape of modern events, global event brands have increasingly leveraged their power and influence to create geo-localized events and virtual conferences, catering to diverse audiences around the world. This approach has not only democratized access to information and opportunities but also fostered a sense of inclusivity and connectedness that transcends geographical boundaries.

The power of global event brands lies in their ability to blend global reach with local relevance. Through the strategic use of experiences and technology, these brands can host events that are simultaneously accessible to a global audience and tailored to the specific cultural and regional nuances of different locales. This dual approach ensures that participants feel a deeper connection and engagement with the event content, regardless of where they are.

For example, major events or exhibitions like the music festival Tomorrow Land or the trade fair Big5 Global have perfected the art of geo-localization or virtualization. While they attract attendees from around the globe to their main event, they also host satellite events in various countries, each tailored to the local ecosystem. These localized events offer region-specific insights, showcase local values, and address market-specific challenges, all while maintaining the overarching global narrative of innovation and technology.

Virtual conferences have further revolutionized this concept. Events like TEDx, which started as independently organized local events under the TED brand, have become a global phenomenon. The use of in-person events and virtual platforms allows for simultaneous global participation, with localized content and speakers. This not only broadens the reach but also enriches the content by incorporating diverse perspectives and experiences from around the world.

The integration of localization strategies goes beyond content and speakers. It also encompasses the logistical aspects of event planning. Global event brands invest in understanding the cultural preferences, languages, and even the local business etiquette of their target audiences. This meticulous attention to detail ensures that the events resonate deeply with local participants, enhancing their overall experience and satisfaction.

Moreover, the rise of hybrid events, combining in-person and virtual elements, exemplifies the balance between global presence and local engagement. These events offer a physical space for local attendees while simultaneously streaming to a worldwide audience. The physical attendees benefit from direct networking opportunities and the tactile experience of the event, while virtual participants gain access to the same high-quality content and interactions.

Global event brands also play a crucial role in fostering economic development and cultural exchange. By hosting localized versions of their events, they bring international expertise and investment to local markets, stimulating innovation and growth. This cross-pollination of ideas and resources can lead to significant advancements in various industries, benefiting both local and global communities.

A strategic blend of global reach and local relevance has become essential for successful event brands. Take COSMOPROF, the leading B2B global network of events, which harnesses the strengths of two major event players: Informa Markets, the world's largest exhibition organizer, and Bolognafiere, a prominent Italian venue and organizer. This partnership exemplifies the power of combining global scale with local significance, even in B2B events.

By leveraging technology to create geo-targeted events and virtual conferences, these brands have expanded their audiences while enhancing the quality and impact of their events. This approach keeps events relevant, engaging, and transformative, fostering a sense of global community while honoring local diversity. In our increasingly interconnected world, balancing these elements is not just a competitive edge but a necessity for the future of events.

A Strategic Approach to Virtual Events

In the rapidly evolving landscape of event management, virtual events have emerged as a crucial component. As we navigate the complexities of modern technology and the ever-changing needs of our audiences, understanding the strategic importance of virtual events is essential.

This paragraph delves into the strategic approach necessary for effectively incorporating virtual events into our repertoire, highlighting how these digital gatherings can complement and enhance traditional in-person experiences. By situating virtual events within the broader context of our "in-person" industry, we can unlock their potential to create meaningful and impactful connections, even in a world where physical presence is not always possible.

Navigating the complexities of virtual events necessitates a robust strategic approach. In our current landscape, there are no easy solutions, making it vital to understand both the how and why behind the use of virtual events. Establishing context and employing specific frameworks are essential guidelines in this endeavor.

The crucial question in strategy is "why" rather than "what," "when," or "how." Profit is not the "why"; it is a result of our activities. When discussing virtual events, we must have clear in mind that we are entering specific "digital triggers." for this reason we need to use specific strategic framework to better understand this element of digital experience. For this, Gartner's Hype Cycle is a useful concept.

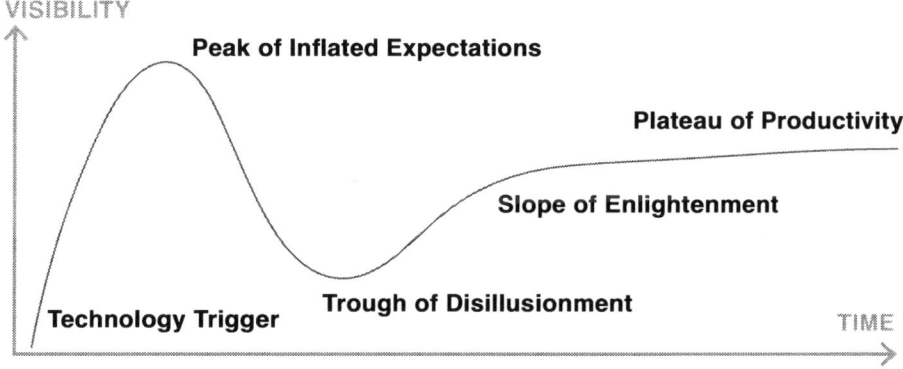

Initially, especially because of the COVID-19 situation, there was a high enthusiasm for virtual events, followed by disillusionment, then enlightenment, and finally, we are entering the phase of productivity. Given time and money constraints, reaching productivity quickly is crucial.

A strategic approach requires a clear framework. One useful framework is the taxonomy of innovation. Digital elements can be categorized into five layers:

LAYER 0: BUILDING BLOCKS:
Identifies the technological blocks, i.e. everything that includes the components that allow the technologies to work (for example, CPUs, sensors, servers, etc.).

LAYER 1: TECHNOLOGIES:
contains current technologies, i.e. the technological elements that can be combined in different ways for a varied set of applications.

LAYER 2: CLUSTERS
These technologies can be grouped into clusters (Level 2), with each cluster organized around/based on a shared technological concept underpinning the technologies in Layer n1, the common technological concept underlying the technologies of the underlying layer.

LAYER 3: APPLICATIONS
The combination of technologies, from one or more clusters, allows different technological applications, which constitute Level 3.

LAYER 4: MACRO-TRENDS/BUSINESS MODEL

Finally, these series of applications could be adapted to implement a specific business model (e.g., Industry 4.0) or define a social/macrotrend (e.g., sharing economy), which belongs to the highest Level 4.

Virtual events fall into the third layer, involving applications—a mix of various technology clusters like augmented reality, virtual reality, machine learning, big data, and artificial intelligence.

The most important layer for strategy is the fourth: macro trends and business models. For virtual events, this means focusing on data monetization rather than just selling space.

Adapting to virtual events and new business models requires understanding our clients' needs, leveraging data, and focusing on creating value for our industry ecosystem. This strategic approach will help us navigate the current chaos and emerge stronger.

The Lindy Effect

The event industry is booming as never before and the sub-sector of exhibitions is growing very fast. For example, the trade fair industry used to be neglected but is now perceived as crucial from the beneficiaries' (visitors and exhibitors) point of view.

But why is this happening? Is there any theory that explains the success of this "old" instrument that we call "live events"? The answer is yes, and I want to share an interesting theory that can be applied to our industry: The Lindy Effect.

The Lindy Effect is a concept that describes the relationship between the age of a thing (or an idea) and its expected lifespan. According to the Lindy Effect, the longer something has been around, the longer it will likely remain relevant and useful. Longevity implies resistance to change, obsolescence, or competition, and greater odds of continued existence into the future.

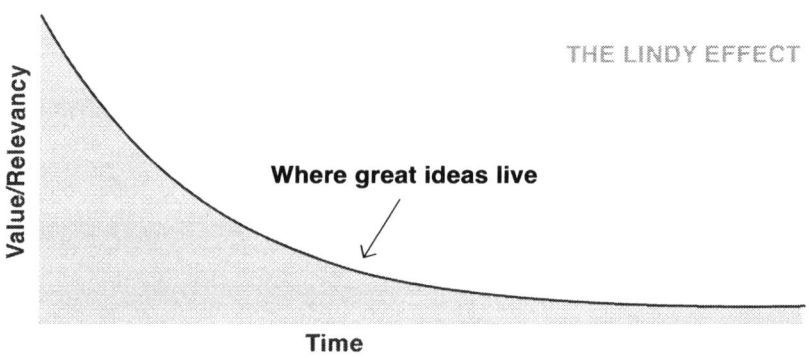

Originally coined by Albert Goldman and later popularized by Nassim Nicholas Taleb, the Lindy Effect suggests that every additional period of survival implies a longer life expectancy. For example, a book that has been in print for 40 years is likely to stay in print for another 40 years.

Events have been around for centuries, serving as platforms for knowledge, socialization, communication, and businesses to showcase their products and services, network, and engage with similar people. This long history indicates that events are resilient and have adapted over time to remain relevant. The Lindy Effect suggests that the longer events continue to thrive, the more likely they are to persist in the future. This endurance is a testament to their inherent value and adaptability in the face of changing market dynamics and technological advancements.

The Lindy Effect can also be used to evaluate the potential success of new events and trends in the industry. If, for example, a new festival or large event has been around for a short time, it is less likely to have proven its staying power and is, therefore, less likely to be successful in the long term. In contrast, an event running for several years has demonstrated its value and resilience, suggesting it will continue to be successful.

The mathematical foundation for the Lindy Effect is based on the concept of power laws. Power laws describe a relationship between two quantities where one quantity varies as a power of the other. The Lindy Effect is closely related to the power-law distribution, which describes the frequency of events that follow a power-law relationship.

In the case of the Lindy Effect, a power-law distribution models the probability distribution of the remaining lifespan of an item. Suppose that the lifespan of an item follows a power-law distribution with a shape parameter of α. Then the probability density function of the remaining lifespan of the item after it has already survived for t units of time can be written as:

$$f(x \mid t) = \alpha t^{\alpha} / x^{\alpha+1}$$
$$f(x \mid t) = \alpha t\alpha/x\alpha+1$$

where x is the remaining lifespan of the item, and t is the time that the item has already survived.

The Lindy Effect suggests that $\alpha\alpha\alpha$ is greater than 1, indicating that the distribution has a long tail. This means the probability of the item surviving for a long time is higher than for a short time. As an item ages, it becomes more embedded in culture or society, and its influence grows, making it more likely to persist.

Understanding the Lindy Effect can provide valuable insights for event organizers. Focusing on longevity is essential; events that have been successful for many years are likely to continue thriving, so prioritize improving and expanding these established events. When evaluating new ventures, be cautious. While innovation is important, newer events may not have the same staying power as established ones. Leveraging established trends and practices that have stood the test of time is also crucial; integrating these into your event planning can ensure long-term success. Finally, aim to make your event a staple within the industry. The more it becomes ingrained in the culture, the more likely it will persist.

The Lindy Effect provides a theoretical foundation for understanding why some events continue to thrive while others do not. By recognizing the value of longevity and the resilience of established events, organizers can better strategize and ensure the continued success and relevance of their exhibitions. In a world of rapid change, the Lindy Effect reminds us that endurance and historical success are strong indicators of future viability.

The Post-COVID-19 Resurgence

The COVID-19 pandemic brought an unprecedented challenge to the event industry, forcing a pause and a reevaluation of the importance of physical gatherings. As the industry rebounds, the eagerness for live events underscores a fundamental human truth - our innate need for direct, human-to-human interaction.

The Lindy Effect previously discussed highlights the fact that events have been around for a long time, and there is no reason to doubt that this will change - no matter how much our society changes due to innovations and revolutions in terms of science and technology.

Events have always been about more than business or entertainment; they are about human connection, shared experiences, and collective envisioning of the future. The digital shift has not diminished this; it has amplified it, allowing us to connect more deeply, share more broadly, and experience more intensely.

Today's event industry is at a pivotal juncture: The digital shift has opened new horizons of possibility, transforming events from periodic gatherings into ongoing, dynamic communities. As we embrace this exciting era, we're not just participating in events; we're part of an ever-evolving story of human connection, one that continues to shape our world and our future.

CHAPTER 12

The Ascendency of Data & the Importance of the "In-Person" Experience

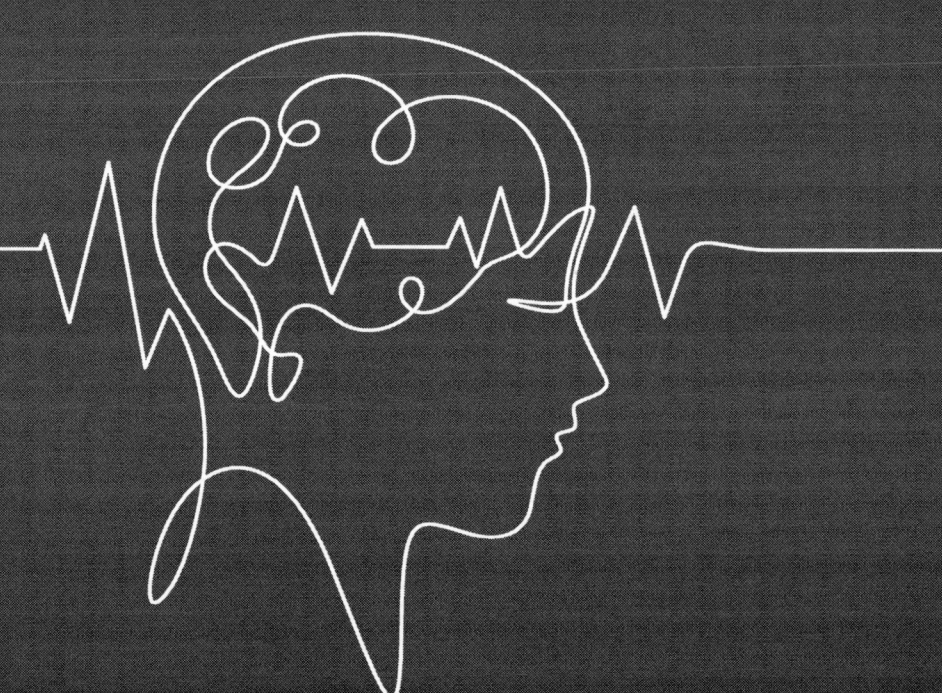

In contemplating the future, it is crucial to comprehend the present landscape. Contemporary thinkers highlight our era as one of significant transition, moving away from the entrenched ideologies those powerful "isms" that shaped the 20th century toward a new paradigm dominated by data. This chapter explores the increasing centrality of data and its profound implications for the future of events, examining this shift from multiple perspectives.

In contemplating the future, it is crucial to comprehend the present landscape. Contemporary thinkers highlight our era as one of significant transition, moving away from the entrenched ideologies—those powerful "isms" that shaped the 20th century—toward a new paradigm dominated by data. This chapter explores the increasing centrality of data and its profound implications for the future of events, examining this shift from multiple perspectives.

From Ideologies to Data:
A Paradigm Shift

As we reflect on the 20th century, a period rich with idealism, it becomes evident that what we now call ideologies once functioned as secular religions. Influential thinkers like Descartes and the Enlightenment philosophers ushered in an age of reason, diminishing the central role of traditional religion in favor of ideologies. These ideologies didn't arise in a vacuum; they were forged in the crucible of historical events and human interactions.

The three primary ideologies of the 20th century, fascism, capitalism, and communism, each offered distinct visions for society.

Fascism emphasized the collective good over individualism, promoting a vision of national and communal strength. However, the implementation of fascist ideals often led to authoritarian regimes, with Nazism under Hitler being the most notorious example. While fascism promoted community and national unity, its application frequently resulted in oppression and conflict, leading to its decline.

Communism, with its egalitarian principles, sought to create a society where all individuals were equal, sharing both responsibilities and rewards. The ideal of communal living and collective ownership promised a utopian vision of human equality. However, communism's centralized decision-making proved inefficient, as exemplified by the challenges in setting prices and managing economies through rigid, predetermined rules. The market's dynamic nature often outpaced the slower, bureaucratic mechanisms of communist states.

Capitalism, on the other hand, thrived on individualism and personal initiative. It encouraged people to pursue their happiness and forge their paths, fostering innovation and rapid adaptation to changing conditions. The market's flexibility allowed for real-time adjustments, such as fluctuating prices within a single city. This system's efficiency and responsiveness contributed to its dominance in the post-war world, especially as fascism waned and communism struggled.

Recent decades have witnessed humanity's gradual departure from the ideologies that once defined global discourse. This shift, alongside advances in computational technology, has positioned data at the forefront of power and influence. The decline of major ideological "isms" from the 20th century, such as socialism, communism, and fascism, and the complexities within capitalism, mark this transition. Capitalism, despite its dominance, faces scrutiny as its foundational principle—that money drives everything—undergoes profound reevaluation. The abundance of money has not resolved deeper, fundamental issues, leading to a critical reassessment of capitalism's sustainability, especially in the face of ecological crises and human happiness.

In this post-ideological era, machines capable of processing vast amounts of data have created a new value system. Collecting, analyzing, and leveraging data now surpasses traditional forms of control, ushering in new "ideological doctrines" centered on what could be called "dataism". This emerging paradigm influences the present and will undoubtedly shape the future, but to what extent is yet to be determined.

To understand the rise of dataism, we must first delve into the concept of ideologies. Humans, as storytellers, create narratives that evolve into perceived realities. Consider soccer: individuals from diverse backgrounds—be it a Congolese, Japanese, Filipino, or Indian—can gather and play soccer, understanding the basic rules despite never having met. These rules, such as scoring goals and using feet, are not tangible realities but shared stories that have gained universal acceptance. This phenomenon illustrates how humans create and embrace shared constructs. We use those constructs to work and play with each other across the world - no matter what language we speak, religion we believe in, or any other factor.

Another example is McDonald's. What defines McDonald's? It's not the hamburgers, the stores, the employees, or the owners—each of these elements can change. McDonald's is a concept, a story built over decades, recognized globally. No matter where you go, you know that the experience of eating at a McDonald's will share many of the same qualities. This narrative is so ingrained that it shapes our understanding of reality, demonstrating the power of collective belief in human-created stories.

The Emergence of Dataism

As we shift from these traditional constructs, the focus moves toward data. Dataism represents a new ideological framework where data is the primary driver of decision-making and power. Unlike previous ideologies rooted in human narratives, dataism relies on the objective collection and analysis of information. This shift has profound implications for how we organize societies, conduct business, and even perceive reality.

Dataism challenges the existing paradigms by providing a more objective basis for decisions. However, it also raises ethical and philosophical questions about privacy, control, the nature of knowledge, and the validity of the data source. As we navigate this transition, understanding the interplay between data and traditional ideologies will be crucial in shaping a future that balances technological advancements with human values.

As traditional ideologies fade, data has emerged as the new locus of power and influence. Modern titans like Elon Musk, Mark Zuckerberg, and Jeff Bezos do not merely run companies; they manage vast troves of data. This shift reflects a profound transformation in how we understand and navigate the world.

Dataism posits that data is the ultimate source of truth and decision-making. We trust data over opinions, relying on devices and apps to provide insights into our health, habits, and behaviors. This reliance on data is shaping a new kind of belief system where algorithms and analytics guide our choices. In this framework, access to and control of data translate into unprecedented power, capable of solving complex problems and unlocking new possibilities. Data is elevated to an almost sacred status, guiding decisions and shaping directions across all levels of society.

Entities that command vast reservoirs of data wield immense power, fundamentally altering social and economic landscapes. These 'data masters' influence politics, economics, and culture through their control of information. This dynamic is evident in our daily lives, manifested through ubiquitous technologies like smartphones and other integrated devices. These technologies thrive on data usage, exchange, and predictive management, often anticipating our needs and preferences better than we can ourselves. This capability reinforces the perception of data as a new form of religion or deep creed, central to modern life.

Our interactions with machines, particularly through artificial intelligence (AI) and machine learning, harness the power of data in unprecedented ways. These technologies promise significant benefits, simplifying our lives and addressing complex challenges. However, they also portend a future where a handful of entities might control most global data, raising critical questions about power distribution and societal impact.

The traditional role of states, which have historically been central to community identity and governance, now contends with supra-national entities possessing greater power and influence. Technological giants like Microsoft, Amazon, Meta, Alibaba, and Baidu transcend national boundaries, fostering new forms of identity that surpass the historical empires that have shaped humanity over millennia.

The Role of Data
in Co-Creating Value

In the context of the event industry, this data-centric approach is revolutionizing how events are conceived and executed. Consider Amazon's vision of bringing together suppliers and customers in one place to foster collaboration and innovation. This concept underscores the value of data-driven interactions, where insights derived from data enhance the effectiveness and impact of events.

Similarly, Facebook and other tech giants recognize the power of in-person gatherings. Despite their vast digital reach, they understand that real magic happens when people meet face-to-face, sharing their passions and goals. These interactions generate valuable data, further fueling the cycle of innovation and improvement.

Data has become the lifeblood that informs every aspect of planning and execution within the current event industry. Insights derived from data drive decision-making and strategy, enabling event organizers and tech companies to co-create value. This data-centric approach optimizes attendee, sponsor, and exhibitor experiences, ensuring seamless and intuitive interactions.

Event technology companies play a crucial role in this ecosystem, collaborating with organizers to deliver engaging and valuable experiences. By leveraging data, these partnerships enhance the frontstage and backstage aspects of events, maximizing engagement and creating meaningful connections.

The transition to dataism represents a profound shift in our worldview, where data is the cornerstone of modern life. This new doctrine influences every sector, reshaping social, economic, and political landscapes. Understanding and navigating this data-centric era requires recognizing its potential and addressing its challenges, ensuring that the power of data is harnessed for the greater good. The event industry, as a microcosm of this broader trend, exemplifies how data can create value and foster human connection in a rapidly evolving world.

Ethical Considerations and Privacy Concerns

The widespread collection and utilization of data raise critical ethical and privacy concerns. Privacy is increasingly blurred as individuals often relinquish personal data without full awareness or consent. This scenario necessitates a thorough examination of who owns and controls this information.

The current system, rooted in a concept of "ownership" that is already evolving, prompts us to question the true motives behind these new "global empires." Are they driven by the welfare of individuals, the interests of corporate owners, or the benefit of the corporations themselves—entities where the human element is increasingly diluted?

New technologies, particularly Blockchain, are emerging to ensure data ownership decentralization. This technology integrates into a complex and evolving landscape where multiple technologies—AI, blockchain, quantum computing, and bioengineering—are moving from experimental stages to practical applications. These technologies are converging, suggesting that they will soon coalesce into a unified, transformative force.

The future will see a significant shift in the responsibility of those who own data. As we develop technologies more intelligent than ourselves, particularly in AI, the role of those who can gather and analyze data must transcend mere profit motives. This shift must prioritize the greater good of humanity. Artificial intelligence, while powerful, lacks emotional intelligence and intuition—qualities that remain essential in our daily lives. As we delve deeper into this digital era, mediated by advanced AI tools, we face new challenges.

Imagine receiving a call from a loved one that perfectly mimics their voice and image but is entirely generated by AI. The distinction between reality and artificiality will blur, making it crucial to navigate these advancements thoughtfully and ethically.

Data and the Evolution of Events

Data's growing importance is reshaping the labor market and social structures. Professions in data analysis and AI are becoming central, while others may become obsolete, exacerbating inequality. It is crucial to avoid a simplistic "human vs. machine" dichotomy. Technology is an integral part of humanity, and rather than viewing it as a threat, we should see it as an extension of human capability.

We may witness a future where a small group of individuals advance themselves through access to advanced technologies, creating a new form of "humanity." This scenario involves AI interfacing with bioengineering enhancements, leading to a profound division in society. A tiny proportion of "Homo sapiens" could evolve into "homo sapiens +"—individuals who seamlessly integrate technologies into their biological systems. These enhancements would augment basic life functions and thought processes, fundamentally altering what it means to be human.

As we navigate the rise of dataism, we must address the ethical implications it brings. The convergence of advanced technologies offers immense potential but also poses significant challenges. By thoughtfully integrating these technologies and prioritizing the collective good, we can harness the power of data to create a more equitable and advanced society. The event industry, as a microcosm of these broader trends, exemplifies how data can drive innovation and foster meaningful human connections in an ever-evolving world.

Events have always been pivotal in driving technological, social, and economic evolution. Historically, as we have seen, large events and exhibitions have served as crucial collective moments where specialized niches converge to envision and co-create the future. These gatherings provide a platform for communities and experts in specific niches and fields to share, engage, and collaborate in profoundly human and interactive ways.

For instance, exhibitions, as hubs of innovation and co-creation, acquire even greater importance in the data-driven era. They are not merely showcases for the latest innovations but also arenas for authentic human interaction—a rarity in our increasingly digital world dominated by AI and technological mediation (mainly through screens today). Authenticity and reality, inherent to exhibitions, become unique competitive advantages in an age where digital experiences can be easily manipulated.

The inability to distinguish between true and false digital experiences threatens the core value of social and economic relationships: trust. Non-replicable physical experiences, such as those provided by events, large gatherings, and exhibitions, emphasize the irreplaceable importance of human contact and face-to-face networking. These elements are fundamental for sharing, co-creation, and innovation, and they cannot be counterfeited or falsified by AI.

In the short term, the event industry, and in particular the role of the exhibition industry, must strengthen its narrative around authenticity and real innovation. Events must position themselves as epicenters of authenticity, where passions, thoughts and innovations are not only showcased but lived and experienced in tangible ways.

To achieve this, the industry must focus on creating a sense of community and belonging around events and brands. The events should become platforms for building communities, and promoting long-term exchange and collaboration among participants. The ritual of physical interaction, central to human history, will enhance the significance and value of these events.

A strategic vision centered on authenticity, co-creation, and positive impact can enable events to thrive, becoming focal points for responsible innovation and professional growth. In a world where information can be easily manipulated, physical events offer an authentic stage for sharing real ideas and innovations.

As we navigate the rise of dataism, the role of events becomes increasingly vital. They serve as bastions of authenticity and human interaction in a digital age. By fostering real connections and genuine innovation, "in-person" events can continue to drive progress and maintain trust in an era of unprecedented technological change.

Events as Predictors of Modern Markets

A significant shift in the future events industry is recognizing that gatherings and live events will play a critical role in reducing uncertainty and complexity through data and information management. They bridge the gap between the purely digital and the purely human.

As we extend the trajectory of events into the future, their role evolves from a simple place of facilitators for thoughts, passion, knowledge, and experiences, to true market oracles. With the integration of data and their ritualistic nature, events become central engines of entire industries. They offer a unique perspective by combining human interactions with data analysis, enabling them to anticipate and guide market trends.

Events possess unique characteristics as large collective moments where all participants act as "resource integrators" of data. They contribute to the generation of mutual value and services, exchanging values, goods, and information, independently by the nature of the event.

Applying the pervasive concepts of AI to individual niches reveals that events are the cornerstone of gatherings, uniquely bringing together a complex set of hyper-vertical passions, competencies, and knowledge from both the demand and supply sides. The quality of participants and the volume of data, information, and interactions make events pivotal in transforming from business enablers to driving forces of the market they are in, or "market oracles," as I prefer to call them.

The concept of feed-forward introduces substantial innovation. Unlike the inefficiency of current event archiving data modes, feed-forward leverages real-time data algorithms for computational efficiency. For instance, the entry or registration phase of an event, often considered trivial,

becomes a significant opportunity for profiling and certi-
fying participants, sponsors, and exhibitors. The reactions
and the interaction during the event is the vital strength to
anticipate and understand the future. These interactions,
integrated with other data across show phases, deepen
the understanding of each industry's unique elements.

STRATEGIC QUESTIONS FOR EVENT ORGANIZERS

Every event organizer must clarify their strategic direction in
a data-centric evolution by asking: "Who can bring together
under one roof so many hyper-specific and coherent people?"

Despite AI advancements, no element surpasses the importance of physical interaction, giving events a competitive advantage and a strong and unique new narrative:
Events are real and cannot be faked. This advantage and
this new narrative must be defended, cultivated, and shared with all the stakeholders. The era of deep fakes, fake
news, and so on is already here and in-person events are
a strong and fundamental asset for trust, connection and
the assurance of the reality of what one is seeing.

This uniqueness of the event industry serves as the pivot
for developing new systems using next-generation Data
Intelligence technologies to predict market trends. Algorithms, operating in a predictive mode, can anticipate market dynamics rather than merely react to them.

Events will increasingly function as data extraction platforms, maintaining continuous contact with participants.
Through granular, pervasive, and continuous behaviors,
participants provide all the elements necessary for generating value within an entire market niche.

The evolution of events from service centers focused on
experience interactions to oracle ecosystems capable of
predicting sector performance marks a significant transformation. These ecosystems will build relationships between
previously unknown tribes of counterparts of different people to the available data and continuous interactions, solidifying events as indispensable oracles of modern markets.

From "Archive" to "Oracle"

Traditionally, events have operated in an "archive" mode, collecting and analyzing existing or historical behaviors through registration data, on-site movement, expenditure on the venues, lead generation interactions, event apps, customer insights, and business intelligence.

This approach, while efficient, primarily serves an "ex-post" need, focusing on past and present information.

However, the future of events lies in transitioning to a "near-time" or "oracle" mode. This shift involves optimizing information about future events, allowing organizers to shape them in the present. By engaging and managing relationships with beneficiaries—primarily visitors, sponsors, and exhibitors—through predictive listening and integration with historical databases, events can analyze ongoing scenarios and work with hyper-specialized information from the future.

Event organizers are becoming more advanced in collecting data through registration, event apps, and shared content. This data, coupled with interactions and insights, positions organizers to step beyond their traditional role of merely gathering people. They can become the oracle of their niche, intercepting and understanding future trends and directions.

The ability to gather people and leverage technology to collect data and insights transforms organizers into more than operational facilitators. They become capable of predicting the future and guiding their industry. Data has the power to elevate events from "archive" mode to "oracle" mode, providing foresight into where everything is heading.

In a post-digital world, moving from feedback-based past analyses to feed-forward future predictions marks a significant transformation. Events, through this shift from "archive" to "oracle," can harness data's full potential to anticipate and shape the future of their industries. By balancing technological advancements with human interactions, exhibitions will continue to thrive as engines of innovation and progress.

Examples of predictive approaches abound in various sectors, such as predictive maintenance in the mechanical world. Within the event industry, providers of traditional experiences or products are evolving into new formats that leverage computing power with an oracle vision. This enables events to anticipate trends and update future scenarios through machine learning and predictive analysis and serve the suppliers of the industry in a new and more advanced role.

Looking ahead, the challenge will be to balance emerging technologies with the need for event organizers to maintain their core mission. Organizers must increasingly rely on and support specialized entities and suppliers for technological and data-oriented aspects. This balance will maximize the impact and effectiveness of events while preserving the authenticity and power of face-to-face interactions, with data taking on a central role.

CHAPTER 13

The Future of Events & The Events of the Future

This final chapter marks the culmination of our journey to understand the profound connection and indelible relationship between human evolution and the world of events. We now turn our focus to envisioning the "future" of events and their evolving role in society.

Envisioning the future is fraught with dynamics and uncertainties, yet it remains a compelling endeavor. Leading futurists often echo the sentiment, "The further back you can look, the further forward you are likely to see." This perspective underscores the importance of history, not as a mere study of the past but as an exploration of the changes that have shaped the paths leading to our present and future.

We are now entering a historical period characterized by unprecedented rapid change. This is why a big part of this book is based on understanding the mechanisms of the past: those changes are crucial to better comprehending the present and anticipating the future. The massive digital transformation underway is one of the most significant evolutions in human history. This transformation, much like previous shifts where humans and technology evolved together, owes much to the pivotal role of meetings, events, and exhibitions.

This epochal moment is akin to the transitions that took Homo sapiens from hunters to farmers or the industrial revolution that redefined the socio-economic landscape. As we navigate this new era, it is essential to approach the future with humility and caution. This chapter aims to provide reflections on the strategic choices that event organizers must consider oreseeing their evolving role within the broader trajectory of humanity and events.

In contemplating the future of events and the events of the future, we explore how they will continue to serve as vital conduits for innovation, connection, and transformation. This exploration is not just about predicting trends but about understanding the underlying forces that will shape the future. By doing so, we can better prepare for the challenges and opportunities that lie ahead, ensuring that events remain central to the human experience.

Events will endure because they are intrinsic to human nature. From ancient times to the present, events have retained essential characteristics: gathering, sharing, connecting, and co-creating. However, as our technology, minds, and consciousness evolve, so too will the nature of these gatherings.

Events in Fully Digital Realities

With the advent of fully digital reality spaces, such as Meta's Metaverse, a new frontier for events is emerging. The Metaverse offers intriguing possibilities for expanding and enhancing the power of events. While some events may fully embrace virtual environments, it is unlikely that the metaverse will become the sole venue for all events. Specific types of events, particularly those involving tangible experiences—such as immersive listening, drink tastings, or examining large machinery—require physical presence and interaction.

Augmented reality (AR) and the metaverse can significantly enhance the event experience, providing new layers of engagement before, during, and after physical gatherings. These technologies can offer immersive previews and detailed follow-ups, enriching the overall experience. However, a full event conducted solely in the metaverse might not capture the sophistication and complexity of traditional in-person events.

While virtual events can be valuable, especially for specific niches, they cannot fully replace the nuanced human experience of physical gatherings. The essence of an event involves more than just visual and auditory stimuli; it encompasses the energy, emotions, and spontaneous interactions that occur in a shared physical space.

Even as figures like Mark Zuckerberg champion the metaverse, its widespread adoption and integration into daily life remain uncertain. The current technology may not yet fully capture the breadth of human experience, but future developments could bring us closer. Just as the phone became ubiquitous, the metaverse might eventually play a more significant role in how we interact. However, it will likely serve as an enhancement rather than a replacement for in-person events.

Technology-Assisted Spontaneous Events

With the rapid advancement of technology, it has become increasingly easy for people to create and attend events. In the future, we can expect spontaneous events to occur more frequently as individuals find common interests.

Imagine a scenario where five people, ifty people, or five thousand people realize they share a passion and decide to meet up spontaneously. Technology will facilitate these spontaneous gatherings by connecting like-minded individuals quickly and efficiently.

For example, wearable technology, such as rings that track health metrics, are becoming more common. These devices provide valuable data, such as blood pressure, body temperature, and sleep patterns, and allow users to share this information with others. It is the same with mindfulness apps and communities. In the future, technology could suggest in-person meetings for people with similar health challenges or interests, enabling them to connect physically. This integration of digital and physical experiences will create spontaneous, meaningful interactions based on shared data and interests.

Gamification & Festivalization

As time becomes an increasingly scarce resource, incorporating elements of gamification into events will enhance the overall experience. Gamification transforms mundane activities into engaging ones by introducing game-like elements such as points, prizes, and interactive challenges. This approach can make even the most boring conferences enjoyable.

For example, the gamification of events could turn a cardiology conference into an engaging experience by incorporating elements like treasure hunts or interactive games. Participants might earn points or rewards for attending sessions, answering questions, or participating in activities. This transformation ensures that attendees are not only informed but also entertained.

Gamification is already prevalent in digital environments, such as video games where users purchase virtual items like skins or accessories. This trend will likely extend to physical events, where attendees can wear event-branded items or earn unique accessories through participation. The blending of digital and physical experiences through incorporating elements traditionally found in video games will create a richer, more engaging event environment.

Being a father of two amazing girls born in 2012 and 2014, I imagine them going to a concert and interacting with friends and peers around the world through a near-future digital realm. I can see that the live in-person experience will likely contain some physical and digital game-like features that will perhaps allow them to get some points and then upgrade to a better location, such as a golden circle near the stage, or they can earn and spend reward points on an exclusive drink or other unique experience.

Alongside gamification, I see the festivalization of events becoming increasingly important. Even industry-specific events, such as automotive retail shows, will incorporate festival-like elements to make them unique and enjoyable.

This approach harkens back to the earliest times of human gatherings, which were often celebratory and festive, involving music, dance, and communal activities.

In the future, events will continue to embrace this spirit of celebration. While modern events may not involve the same level of indulgence in alcohol or substances, they will still aim to evoke high levels of excitement and engagement. Offering and engaging in dopamine-inducing activities, immersive experiences, and interactive elements will create an atmosphere of joy and connection, mirroring the festival-like atmosphere of ancient gatherings.

From Isolation to Connection

Events are growing in importance globally, a trend accelerated by the social distancing and lockdown measures imposed during the COVID-19 pandemic. But, because of the isolation experienced and this new way of working at home, people have realized the significant value of social gatherings, and the event industry is booming as a result. The importance of attending events in person has significantly increased, elevating the status of those who participate.

As people become more financially secure and entrepreneurial, the nature of events will evolve. Instead of being separate, infrequent occurrences, I envision that events will become a constant presence in our lives. With more people working independently or running their own businesses, there will be a greater need for social interaction and shared experiences that niche events focused on specific interests can offer. Otherwise, without these regular ritualistic meetings and collaborations, we would be too isolated. As more and more people do their work primarily from their home and their laptops, the need for using the internet and social media to facilitate physical meet-ups becomes even greater.

In this future, the increased fragmentation of life into more and more unique and possible solitary activities will give rise to more frequent and varied gatherings. These events will cater to diverse interests and passions, providing opportunities for people to connect, share, and celebrate together. The human desire for social interaction and connection will drive the continuous evolution and proliferation of events, making them an integral part of everyday life.

For a current example of the immense power of events inspired by a single individual that brings an increasingly digital younger generation together to participate in a festival-like experience, we can look at the 2024 Taylor Swift tour of concerts. The high ticket prices for her concerts, such as $2,000 for a basic ticket in New York, reflect the immense value people place on being there in person. This phenomenon, known as the Taylor Swift Effect, demonstrates how in-person events drive significant economic and cultural impact.

Taylor Swift's fans, known as "Swifties," create a ripple effect of engagement and purchasing decisions, a phenomenon known as social contagion. The network effect extends her influence beyond individual actions, as fans influence each other, amplifying the impact of her endorsements and appearances. Swift's devoted fan base drives cultural and economic trends, translating their enthusiasm into tangible benefits for associated brands and organizations, showcasing fandom as a force. Additionally, her presence in various domains, such as sports and fashion, generates buzz and drives engagement beyond her music, demonstrating the power of cross-promotion.

Political events, such as the Republican and Democratic National Conventions in the US, also demonstrate the energy and excitement generated by in-person gatherings. The palpable energy at such events is reminiscent of ancient gatherings, like those in the Colosseum or the Greek theater, where people experienced catharsis through shared drama and comedy. In ancient Greece, theatergoers experienced cathartic moments, solving personal problems through the shared experience of tragedy on stage. This theatrical energy, present in political rallies today, highlights a form of collective emotional catharsis and expression that simply cannot occur when everyone is sitting at home behind a laptop and forced to interface through a chat box.

Hyper-Segmentation
of the Event Experience

In the future, the landscape of events will likely encompass both large, mega-events and smaller, exclusive gatherings. We are moving toward a hyper-segmentation of events and experiences, where there will be grand, large-scale events for specific niches, complemented by more precise, tailored experiences within those niches.

For instance, while a major Comic-Con event may attract thousands of fans, there could be sub-events dedicated to specific interests, such as Marvel or even more niche gatherings for Spider-Man enthusiasts. This trend is already evident in the increasing variety and pricing tiers of event packages, from basic to VIP and beyond.

Future events will see even more refined segmentation, with some large events becoming invitation-only. The importance of brand authenticity will also grow, with events becoming powerful brand experiences. TEDx, for example, is already known for its authentic and high-quality presentations. Similarly, brands like Taylor Swift and Cirque du Soleil offer predictable, high-value experiences. This trend will extend to business-to-business (B2B) and government events, where brand reputation will assure attendees of a certain level of quality and engagement. For instance, attending a MarmoMac exhibition in Verona, Italy, in the marble industry carries the assurance of a valuable experience due to the brand's established reputation. This exhibition is a wonderful example of how a "b2b" heavy event (machinery for the marble industry) can become an incredible moment where business meets art meets design, both in the beauty of the event and in the host city at the same time.

The In-Person Experience: Human Connection

The in-person experience is becoming the ultimate, the greatest, and perhaps the most exclusive human interaction. People attend events not just for the content but for the total experience—the journey, the environment, and the escape from their ordinary lives. This desire for authentic human connection will persist, even as technology advances.

While future technology may eventually create virtual experiences that feel almost real, they will still be imitations of true physical encounters. In-person interactions encompass the full spectrum of human connection, including subtle elements like touch, smell, and the shared presence that technology cannot fully replicate. The physical experience offers a richness and authenticity that remains unparalleled.

Consider, for example, physical intimacy. Despite the availability of advanced virtual tools, the tangible presence of another person adds an irreplaceable dimension to the experience. The touch, the scent, the shared breath—all these factors contribute to a deeper connection that technology alone cannot provide.

This exclusive nature of in-person experiences will become even more pronounced as technology advances. In a future where travel may become too expensive or impractical, the ability to meet face-to-face will be cherished even more. Historical moments of human connection, such as peace treaties forged through direct dialogue, highlight the irreplaceable value of in-person interactions.

The power of in-person meetings is evident in significant political gatherings like the G7 or G8 summits. World leaders meet in person to build trust and negotiate crucial decisions. The surge in attendance at political rallies also underscores people's desire for genuine, unmediated experiences.

In-person interactions offer a level of trust and authenticity that digital mediums struggle to match. This growing mistrust of purely digital interactions emphasizes the need for physical presence to maintain genuine connections.

As we look to the future, it is clear that in-person experiences will remain a cornerstone of human interaction. They will become increasingly exclusive and valuable, offering a profound sense of connection that transcends technological limitations. In a world dominated by digital interfaces, the unmediated human touch will be more treasured than ever.

I already shared this previously, but it is so important that I want to reinforce this element: the era of fake news, fake digital experiences, and all the things that will happen with the exponential growth of AI, will put the live in-person experience front and center for the future of the humankind. Real events cannot be faked.

The Importance of Authenticity, Intimacy & Sensory Experience

The concept of authenticity is paramount as we navigate a world where the lines between reality and illusion become increasingly blurred. Events, by their very nature, offer a unique space where we can distinguish and immerse ourselves in reality. They are not just gatherings but profound rituals that fulfill our innate need to connect and engage with one another in a genuine setting.

The organization of an event itself must also embody this authenticity. The experience should be holistic, encompassing the entire journey from leaving home to participating in the event. It should offer a space where emotional connections can flourish, transcending mere transactional interactions. This shift towards a more humanistic and holistic approach will redefine the nature of events, placing greater emphasis on spiritual and emotional connections.

In the future, events will evolve to provide richer, more immersive sensory experiences. Consider the sensory impact of a visit to an Abercrombie store in the 90s, where the strong cologne created a memorable and distinctive atmosphere. Similarly, future events will harness the power of sensory stimuli—sound, smell, touch, and perhaps even taste—to create lasting impressions.

Events already incorporate sensory elements to some extent, as seen in major World Expos or the Olympics, where specific songs or scents can evoke powerful memories even years later. Studies have shown that certain smells can trigger deep, primal responses, highlighting the importance of sensory experiences in creating memorable events. For instance, the smell of rubber tires might be unremarkable or unpleasant to most, but for those in the automotive industry, it can evoke a sense of familiarity and even success.

Understanding the sensory preferences and experiences of attendees will be crucial in designing future events. Organizers will need to create environments that resonate with the specific needs and emotions of their audience, enhancing the overall experience and fostering deeper connections.

As we move forward, the in-person experience will become the ultimate and most exclusive form of human interaction. The combination of authenticity, emotional connection, and immersive sensory experiences will define the future of events. By embracing these elements, we can ensure that events remain meaningful and impactful, offering unparalleled opportunities for human connection and engagement in an increasingly digital world.

The in-person event experience is set to become the ultimate and most exclusive form of human interaction. As such, understanding the participants and tailoring the event to their needs and preferences will be crucial. Event organizers must delve deep into data to create an overall experience that enhances the in-person element to its fullest potential. There is an incredible need in the event industry for research, for deep diving on the visitors' expectations, and for measurement of the Return of Investment for sponsors and stakeholders in general.

Creating a bespoke experience means that organizers control every sensory aspect of the event, ensuring it is memorable and unique. This requires leveraging data for profit and craft an unforgettable experience that attendees will cherish. The goal is to make people want to be part of the event because it makes them feel good and offers a one-of-a-kind experience.

The Soul of Future Events: Connection & Inspiration

In the future, events will continue to be vital for human connection. These gatherings will not only allow individuals to feel the collective energy but also to share experiences with family and close ones. The ability to gather with loved ones and colleagues will make these events even more significant.

As we look ahead, the importance of creating spaces for human gathering will grow. These events will offer opportunities for deep emotional connections, enriching our lives and fostering a sense of community. The energy and authenticity of in-person experiences will remain unmatched, making them indispensable in an increasingly digital world.

The future of events lies in their ability to provide exclusive, premium experiences that cannot be replicated virtually. By focusing on authenticity, sensory engagement, and deep emotional connections, events will continue to play a crucial role in human society, driving cultural and economic impact.

Events have always inspired generations, serving as platforms for individuals to see, co-create, and share the future. This fundamental role will only deepen in the future. Historical figures like Nikola Tesla, who was inspired by the Expos and events he attended as a child, illustrate the profound impact such gatherings can have on brilliant minds. The tactile, real-world experiences provided by events are crucial, especially for the younger generation, who crave physical interaction beyond the screen. These experiences foster inspiration and curiosity, driving attendees to envision and create the future.

The essence of events lies in their ability to bring people together for inspiration and connection. As technology continues to advance, humans will increasingly augment their capabilities with tools like phones, AirPods, and wearable tech. However, the core human need for soul-to-soul connection will remain unchanged. Events will continue to be the venues where people gather, not just to use technology, but to connect with other humans on a deeper level. This connection will be the driving force behind the inspirational power of events, making them even more significant in the future.

The Continually Evolving Nature of Events

As we look towards the future, it is clear that the role of events will continue to evolve, driven by advancements in technology and changes in human behavior. The in-person experience, with its unmatched authenticity and depth of connection, will remain the pinnacle of human interaction. Despite the rise of digital and virtual environments, the need for physical gatherings will persist, offering unique opportunities for genuine engagement and inspiration.

The future will see a diverse landscape of events, ranging from grand, large-scale gatherings to smaller, highly personalized experiences. This hyper-segmentation will cater to the specific needs and interests of various niches, ensuring that every attendee finds value and relevance. The integration of advanced technologies will facilitate spontaneous events, connecting like-minded individuals in real time and creating new possibilities for social interaction.

Gamification and festivalization will transform how we experience events, making them more engaging and enjoyable. By incorporating elements of play and celebration, even traditionally mundane conferences will become vibrant and memorable occasions. This evolution will rekindle the spirit of ancient gatherings, where communal activities and shared joy were central to the human experience.

As people become more entrepreneurial and financially secure, and as the working experience becomes more isolated,; the nature of events will further adapt to reflect our increased desire for passion and play. Events will become a constant presence, seamlessly integrated into our daily lives, providing continuous opportunities for connection and celebration.

Ultimately, the future of events lies in their ability to blend the digital and physical worlds, creating immersive, authentic experiences that resonate deeply with participants. By focusing on authenticity, sensory engagement, and emotional connection, events will continue to inspire and unite us, playing a crucial role in the social and cultural fabric of our lives.

In this rapidly changing world, the essence of events remains constant: they are the places where we come together to share, to learn, to inspire and be inspired, and to grow. As we embrace new technologies and evolving social dynamics, events will remain the beating heart of human connection, driving innovation and fostering a sense of community that transcends boundaries.

One of the most incredible and mind-blowing experience of my life was when I attended the U2 concert at The Sphere in Las Vegas at the end of 2023. It was also one of the main reasons I decided to write this book. The immersive technology surrounded us, but what truly consumed me were the emotions. I laughed, I sang, I cried, I dreamed. The power of the music, amplified by breathtaking visuals, coursed through my body—a visceral experience I can still feel today. It wasn't just the sensory overload that made it unforgettable; it was sharing that moment with a friend, someone who mirrored my sensitivity and felt the same magic in the air, along with thousands of others in that shared 'mystical' experience. Together, we weren't just spectators—we lived that night. The Sphere isn't just a venue; it's a portal to a future where events are no longer attended but fully inhabited. In that space, I realized that the true future of events lies not only in technology but in how deeply it moves us—our souls, our humanity—and how, when shared, those emotions become eternal.

CONCLUSION

IN-PERSON

As we come to the end of this journey through the unstoppable evolution of events, I hope that something of the grand significance of our human gatherings has been communicated to you, the reader. From the earliest social gatherings of our ancestors to the grand spectacles of modern times, events have played a pivotal role in shaping human history and culture. They have been the crucibles of innovation, the platforms for connection, and the stages for human expression.

The evolution of events, as detailed in the first part of this book, highlights key milestones that have defined our collective experience. We explored the dawn of socialization, the rise of rituals, the grandeur of ancient spectacles, and the transformative power of medieval fairs and Renaissance salons. Each era has left an indelible mark on the way we gather, celebrate, and connect.

In the second part, we delved into the art and science of event organizing. This balance between creativity and logistics is what makes events so special. Personal anecdotes and industry insights underscored the importance of passion, resilience, and strategic thinking in overcoming the myriad challenges event organizers face. The journey of healing and rediscovery through events is a testament to their transformative power.

The digital shift and the impact of COVID-19 have ushered in a new era for the event industry. Technology has redefined how we plan, execute, and experience events. While the integration of digital tools has created new opportunities, it has also reinforced the irreplaceable value of in-person gatherings. Phygital experiences blending physical and digital elements have emerged as a powerful paradigm, yet the heart of any event remains the human connection.

Data has become a cornerstone of the future of events. We are witnessing a paradigm shift from traditional ideologies to a data-driven world. The role of data in co-creating value, shaping societal norms, and driving innovation is profound. However, as we navigate this new landscape, ethical considerations and the need for balanced data usage are paramount.

Looking ahead, the future of events is bright and filled with potential - just as I am an optimist and a firm believer in humanity's ability to overcome obstacles and transform challenges into opportunities. The trends of gamification, festivalization, and hyper-segmentation point to a more personalized and engaging event experience. Yet, the soul of future events will always be about connection and inspiration. Creating meaningful and memorable experiences will remain at the core of successful gatherings, and the advent of AI will only place more importance on meeting in-person.

Those who wish to host, organize, or participate in deeply meaningful, impactful, profitable, successful, and fun events would do well to take the lessons learned from the gatherings of our earliest ancestors and apply them to the events of today and of the future. No matter how much things change, the fundamentals stay the same.

As we conclude, it's crucial to embrace the evolving nature of events and the opportunities they present. The lessons learned from the past can guide us in shaping a future where events continue to be hubs of human connection, learning, and innovation. The energy of gatherings, the authenticity of interactions, and the power of shared experiences will ensure that events remain an integral part of our lives.

So, let us look forward with excitement and anticipation. The future of human gatherings is not just about technological advancements or data-driven insights it's about the timeless power of coming together, celebrating our humanity and the experiences we share, and co-creating a better future.

The "in-person" event bubble is a unique reality that exists in a place beyond space and a location outside of time. And it is within this container that the most important and exciting things happen, where connections are formed, innovations are seeded, and the slow yet gradual evolution of the human collective moves forward, step-by-step. And today, just as it has always been and it always will be, that unstoppable journey happens in-person.

A Conversation
with Julius Solaris

Shortly before the publication of this book, I sat down for a conversation with my friend and colleague Julius Solaris. As a leader in the event industry, I wanted to get his thoughts on some of the most pressing questions and topics. In this chapter, Juluis shares his ideas on the possible future of events, his perspective on AI, current and near-future challenges for the event industry, what is most important in order to host a successful event, and more.

Julius Solaris is a leading figure in the event industry, known for founding Boldpush and EventMB and his work with high-profile technology companies like Swapcard and Hopin. Recognized as a top industry influencer for over a decade, Julius has designed events for 60,000 professionals, conducted groundbreaking research, and delivered keynotes to over 200,000 attendees worldwide. His insights have reached hundreds of thousands through reports, articles, and events.

Enrico Gallorini: In your career, you've witnessed and influenced significant changes in the event industry. How would you describe the evolution of in-person events, especially in the context of technological advancements and the recent rise of virtual and hybrid formats?

Julius Solaris: There's a book to be written just on this topic. The interesting part is that until 2019, it was a different scenario. By the end of 2019, we were peaking towards experiences and in-person events, probably one of the best years ever. How did we get to that point? Through a lot of hustle and a lot of reinvention of the concept of in-person events. Traditionally, the issues until then were the inability to measure, or the extreme difficulty of measuring, what was happening. Obviously, that has changed in the past few years.

Up until then, there was still the conception that events were difficult, complex, and required a lot of work to put together, which is still the case. But making all that work count towards the bottom line, whatever that was, was fairly difficult. And then came the pandemic. The reason why in-person events were so popular in 2019, I think, still persists today. It's the rise of social media and social online interactions essentially having an effect. I'm being more philosophical here since it's for a book, but I think it's interesting. From a certain point of view, the more we interacted online, the more we saw the need to meet in person.

That's something that a lot of people didn't grasp at the time and still do not grasp today. They don't grasp how correlated the growth of social media and the growth of events are. At the beginning of the rise of social media, there was a conception that they were inversely correlated, meaning more social media, fewer events. But the opposite became true. That's my theory; there's no research on this, but I feel like I've seen it.

This was exacerbated during the pandemic with virtual events. If you think of virtual events as a closer, more personal interaction than what you would have on social media, then you see the parallel. Again, we made the same mistake when we saw social networks like Twitter in 2006 or 2007. People were saying, "We're not going to go to events because we're going to be on Twitter."

Then, during the pandemic, it was the same thing with virtual events: "We're not going to go back to in-person events because virtual events are so much better and more convenient for everybody." And then, obviously, the opposite happened. The comeback that we've seen in the past two or three years—nobody expected that level of comeback so fast, with many events going back to 2019 levels, even breaking them in some aspects.

What changed events forever was the realization that it was easier to make money from events and to track what was happening. Technology developed very quickly. The event tech sphere saw more product development in 2021 than in the previous two decades combined. Event tech companies started to launch new features constantly, and that helped to give confidence to a lot of marketing teams, CMOs, and the like to say, "Okay, events work, we know how to measure them."

So, they started transferring what was learned during the pandemic into in-person events, creating programs and seeing the need to go back to in-person gatherings. We're here today with 2024 probably being when we peak that growth. The question now is, what is going to happen afterward? Most research points out that the growth will slow down next year.

Enrico Gallorini: **There are two points I try to highlight in the book. One is the rise of working from home. So, this hyper-isolation that we're having, and will probably continue to have, will increase the need for in-person events. And the other is the growth of AI. With the difficulty of understanding what is true and what is false in digital interactions, the need for events will become even more important.**

What are your thoughts about these two elements? One is the hyper-isolation we're going to have as humanity, and the other is the rise of AI. With the digital transformation and the rise of AI in event planning, what do you foresee as the future role of in-person gatherings? How can they coexist or complement the increasing trend toward virtual experiences?

<u>Julius Solaris</u>: There are two overarching topics when I present about events these days. One is the use of events as the new office. Events become the office for a lot of distributed teams that don't have opportunities to get together. Events are perfect opportunities for this. I started saying it six or nine months ago, and I think just last week or two weeks ago, the Harvard Business Review spoke about events as the new office. So it's good; it's Harvard official now.

But that is what we've seen. Teams, like offices and bosses, are sending 20, 30, 40—I've heard of up to 60 people being sent to one event to have an offsite. These are great opportunities not only to learn but also to network and entertain. Not everybody can afford incentive trips like in the past, so they want to leverage the fact that you're getting a holistic experience with some learning, some entertainment, and some networking. You're ticking all the boxes, so it's the natural step.

I think it's going to go even further. I feel there's a way out for the large inventory of commercial real estate sitting empty in buildings to be repurposed as event space. That could be a very possible scenario in the future. If you look at the downtowns in America, they're essentially empty. All these people that got together at conventions could repopulate the downtowns. What if the space around these convention centers could be repurposed for events?

That's a potential scenario if we go down the route of more work-from-home jobs. Obviously, that trend is present, but more companies are sending people back to the office for two or three days. However, two or three days don't create that five-days-a-week feeling where everyone has to be there. Many team members may be missing, and therefore, events become key to maintaining that connection.

On AI, again, we have the exacerbation of online interaction, whether it is through social media or AI. I've been a proponent, since the beginning of the rise of AI, of this dichotomy: the more we experience online, the more we crave real human interaction. I was checking tools like Google's "Illuminate," for example. It's just incredible—taking a paper and creating a two-voice podcast discussing the paper and providing insights. It feels like an NPR podcast, and it's all computer-generated from a PDF.

What we will value more as a premium experience won't even be about being scared of AI. The premium experience will be the human experience. The more human the experience, the more premium it will be. I realized it myself; I could take all my writings from the past 17 years and turn them into a podcast with my voice without doing anything. So, having Julius in person will be a premium experience for my followers. That's why events are primed to be in a strong position.

Research shows that events are currently the most trusted channel to close business deals. Human connection and interaction can't be faked, and therefore, they are more trusted. It's very intuitive.

Enrico Gallorini: **You've often highlighted the importance of addressing complex issues like sustainability and inclusivity in the event industry. How**

do you think in-person events can be designed to be more sustainable and inclusive, and what challenges does the industry need to overcome to achieve this?

Julius Solaris: Just yesterday, I was talking about this on LinkedIn. I said the events industry needs a better PR agency because there's this perception of it being an overworked, super-stressed, burnt-out profession, often seen as just fun and parties. There's a bigger piece here in terms of elevating the profession by creating clear career paths and identifying clear, business-driven education at the university level.

Associations have done a very poor job for the events industry. This is a fact, not an opinion. They've been commercially driven and more concerned about closing businesses for their existence rather than fostering a culture of support for event professionals. We saw it in action during the pandemic; you can't erase that from our minds. The poor job done until then was exposed during the pandemic. That's undeniable because 70-80% of the industry was told, "You're not necessary, we don't need you, figure something out."

That showed what a poor job was done until then to make professionals count. There's no business code for event professionals in the U.S.; no recognition. My frustration with this doesn't stem from any political gain; I'm not a politician. I've always been out of associations or anything like that. My desire for change comes from the thousands of people who wrote to me over the years, in distress, losing their businesses, leaving the industry forever. We've lost 70% of our people in the past four years. These are people I've shared decades with; they're no longer working in events. They're in real estate or whatever because they can't be bothered. They see it as a vocation but can't continue.

This is a problem if we care about the industry. How do we ensure it goes forward if we don't address these key issues? And the key issues are not only mental health from a personal level but also existential issues like sustainability. I feel the discourse on sustainability is not where it should be. Events are travel-intensive and waste-intensive. There are intrinsic elements that put events in the spotlight as soon as sustainability becomes a crisis that governments will tackle. If governments say, "You can't travel to an event of 20,000-30,000 people anymore because the waste created is too much," what are we going to do?

Enrico Gallorini: What would be your suggestions for the in-person industry, the event industry, to at least take a trajectory of understanding that this could happen? How can the industry prepare itself or protect itself? As someone who has championed event technology, how do you reconcile the growing presence of tech in events with the need for authentic human connection? Is there a balance, and if so, how can it be achieved?

Julius Solaris: We need strong association work to make these items count professionally. For example, if you want to be a Certified Meeting Professional (CMP), you should have to embrace sustainability as a core value. It should be a requirement. We're not doing enough in this regard. We also need strong lobbying from impartial associations. The exhibition industry is more sensitive to this because they are more exposed. For example, the Exhibition Industry Council is doing good work in the U.S., lobbying for it.

We used to have meta-associations like Meetings Mean Business back in the days before the pandemic, but that is now gone. Initiatives like that were very important in creating a perception of the economic contribution that the events industry makes, which is in the trillions, and how it helps destinations to grow. Despite being government-funded, especially here in the U.S., many destinations are very commercially oriented. While I embrace capitalism, this focus on the commercial nature is jeopardizing a lot of potential future growth. We need to shift back to more balance.

Enrico Gallorini: Shifting completely from this topic, what advice would you offer to aspiring event organizers who want to create impactful in-person events in a rapidly changing landscape?

Julius Solaris: I've been thinking about this a lot, and one of the ideas I'm looking at for 2026 is the concept that events are going to people, not people going to events anymore.

There will always be a place for macro events, like the Olympics or the World Cup, which will have protection and very advanced sustainability practices. But for events with 15,000 people or less, I feel these will become increasingly local.

Planners will consciously choose cities with large metro areas that are easily accessible. Events will become experience brands, replicating the same format in different cities. For example, South by Southwest is now happening in London and Sydney. This trend is already taking shape in our industry.

We've seen IBTM in Barcelona, Asia, and America, IMEX in Frankfurt, and Connect Marketplace happening all over the U.S. People don't need to travel to the bigger event; they pick the brand they love and attend locally.

Enrico Gallorini: I know you touch on this concept in the book. There's a section about geocloning the experience, where big brands bring events to the market instead of waiting for the market to come to them.

<u>Julius Solaris</u>: Yes, and it's even beyond geocloning. It's like Disneyland Paris, Disneyland Tokyo, and Disney World. Each is Disney, but with a local flavor. Events now have the potential to become experience brands because there are efficiencies and venues that can roll out these formats in different destinations.

<u>Enrico Gallorini</u>: **Reflecting on your journey, what are some of the most memorable events you've been a part of, and what lessons have they taught you about the power of human gatherings?**

<u>Julius Solaris</u>: When I'm asked this question, I always struggle to answer because it's like picking whether you love your mom or dad more. It depends on the type of experience. Every event has its own uniqueness—whether it's the best trade show, concert, business conference, or tech conference. However, I can tell you the most absurd one I've attended was Tony Robbins' "Unleash the Power Within." It was like doing everything you shouldn't do at an event, yet it worked.

Twelve-hour days with no breaks, two-hour registration lines, freezing cold rooms, people hugging and crying—things you typically avoid at events but were done deliberately there. Despite being unconventional, it was incredibly effective. It taught me that when an event pushes boundaries and doesn't conform to the usual standards, it makes people feel alive. And that's what events should do—make you feel alive.

Julius Solaris Biography

Julius Solaris is regarded as the most influential person in the event industry. He is the founder of Boldpush, a management consultancy agency for the event industry.

He founded EventMB (exit to Skift in 2019) and Showthemes, exit in 2018. He has worked for high-profile technology companies (Swapcard and Hopin) and tech events.

Julius has been named one of the most influential individuals in the meetings industry by many magazines and media for the past 10 years. More recently he has been a Meetings Industry Influencer 2022 by Meetings and Conventions magazine. In 2020, 60,000 event professionals attended events Julius designed.

Julius has conducted some of the most groundbreaking research for the event industry. Over 3,000 events reviewed and 15,000 event professionals interviewed.

Over 300,000 event professionals have downloaded Julius' analysis and reports. 300,000 more read EventMB every month, and over 50,000 event professionals attended Julius'events.

Julius has been a keynote for events in 12 countries and over 200,000 attendees.

Geoff Dickinson Biography

Geoff Dickinson graduated from the University of Birmingham, UK with an LLB Law honours degree. He started his career in publishing with emap in London. He worked on the launch of emap's exhibition business creating a series of highly successful tech events. He moved on to be part of the leadership team that launched Haymarket Exhibitions and BBC Haymarket Exhibitions creating a series of large scale consumer exhibitions.

Geoff worked for a variety of events businesses holding numerous senior roles including being the Global Managing Director of IIR Exhibitions in the mid 90's. He then spent over a decade as an entrepreneur in Dubai launching two successful exhibitions businesses. He sold his first business to Messe Frankfurt and the second to Clarion. In 2010 he returned to the corporate world by joining dmg events for which he currently acts as the global CEO. dmg events is an international events business with offices in ten global cities, operating events in 28 countries. dmg events focus on trade fairs and conferences covering energy, construction, interiors, coatings, hotel & hospitality, food, security, manufacturing, medical and freight. He currently serves as a Vice President on the board of UFI the international industry events association and is a member of their executive team.

In 2021 he was appointed to serve on His Highness Sheikh Mohammed Bin Rashed Al Maktoum's Dubai International Chamber Advisory Council.

Acknowledgements

My heartfelt thanks to Julius Solaris,
Geoff Dickinson, and everyone who contributed
to the making of In-Person.

Your insights and support have been invaluable
in bringing this exploration of the history
and future of events to life.

This book wouldn't have been possible without
your expertise and passion.

APPENDICES

A list of Important Events

In my journey to explore the importance and evolution of events in the human experience, I have attended many fascinating events, festivals, and exhibitions. While there are countless worth mentioning, for those interested in learning more about the events discussed in this book I've included a useful list of important events.

Académie des Sciences (Paris)
(Founded in 1666): A prestigious scientific institution in France that played a key role in promoting scientific research.
https://en.wikipedia.org/wiki/French_Academy_of_Sciences

Akitu Festival (Mesopotamia)
(First celebrated c. 2000 BCE): The Mesopotamian New Year festival, marking the sowing of barley and celebrating the gods.
https://en.wikipedia.org/wiki/Akitu

Artigiano in Fiera (Milan)
(First held in 1996): A major international fair celebrating artisans and craftsmanship from around the world, held annually in Milan.https://artigianoinfiera.it

Automotive Dealer Day (Verona)
(First held in 2003): A B2B event focused on automotive dealership innovation and trends in Verona, Italy.
www.dealerday.it

Automechanika (Frankfurt)
(First held in 1971): The world's leading trade fair for the automotive service industry, showcasing innovations and networking opportunities.
https://automechanika.messefrankfurt.com/frankfurt/en.html

Big 5 Global (Dubai)
(First held in 1980): The largest and most influential construction exhibition, held in Dubai annually.
https://www.thebig5.ae/

Burning Man (USA)
(First held in 1986): A cultural festival celebrating community, art, and self-expression, held annually in Nevada's Black Rock Desert.https://en.wikipedia.org/wiki/Burning_Man

Cannes Film Festival (France)
(First held in 1946): One of the most prestigious film festivals in the world, celebrating international cinema and awarding the Palme d'Or.
https://en.wikipedia.org/wiki/Cannes_Film_Festival

CES (Las Vegas)
(First held in 1967): The world's largest consumer electronics show, where major tech innovations are revealed.
https://www.ces.tech/

COSMOPROF (Global Network)
(First held in 1967): One of the largest beauty and cosmetics networks of shows in the world, held annually in Bologna, Honk Kong, Mumbai, Las Vegas, Miami and Bangkok.
www.cosmoprof.com

Expo 1889 (Paris)
(First held in 1889): Known for the unveiling of the Eiffel Tower, it showcased industrial advancements of the time.
https://en.wikipedia.org/wiki/Exposition_Universelle_(1889)

Expo 1900 (Paris)
(First held in 1900): Celebrated the achievements of the 19th century and highlighted the innovations of the new century.
https://en.wikipedia.org/wiki/Exposition_Universelle_(1900)

Expo2020 (Dubai)
(First held in 2021): A global event connecting minds and fostering innovations for future challenges, delayed by a year due to the pandemic.
https://www.expo2020dubai.com/

EIMA International (Bologna)
(First held in 1969): A global exhibition for agricultural and gardening machinery, held in Bologna, Italy.
www.eimainternational.it

Gallorinata (Arezzo)
(First held in the 20th century): A traditional family gathering event for the Gallorini family, taking place in Arezzo near Florence, Italy.
(No official link)

G7 Conference
(First held in 1975): An annual summit where leaders from the world's largest economies discuss global issues.
https://en.wikipedia.org/wiki/G7

Gitex Global (Dubai)
(First held in 1981): The biggest tech and startup event, showcasing the latest technological innovations and digital trends.
https://www.gitex.com/

Globe Theatre (London)
(First built in 1599): The iconic Elizabethan theater where Shakespeare's plays were performed, pioneering the concept of ticketed events.
https://en.wikipedia.org/wiki/Globe_Theatre

Heb-Sed Festival (Egypt)
(First celebrated c. 3000 BCE): An ancient Egyptian festival to rejuvenate the Pharaoh's strength and reaffirm their authority.
https://en.wikipedia.org/wiki/Sed_festival

Kumbh Mela (India)
(First held c. 7th century CE): A major Hindu pilgrimage and the largest religious gathering of people in the world, held every 12 years at four different river locations in India.
https://en.wikipedia.org/wiki/Kumbh_Mela

MarmoMac (Verona)
(First held in 1961): An international fair dedicated to marble and natural stone industries.
www.marmomac.com

Misteri Eleusini (Greece)
(First celebrated c. 1500 BCE): The Eleusinian Mysteries were

religious rites in ancient Greece celebrating Demeter and Persephone.https://en.wikipedia.org/wiki/Eleusinian_Mysteries

Monza Formula 1 (Italy)
(First held in 1950): The Italian Grand Prix held at Monza is one of the oldest and most prestigious races in the Formula 1 calendar.https://en.wikipedia.org/wiki/Italian_Grand_Prix

Oktoberfest (Germany)
(First held in 1810): The world's largest beer festival, celebrated annually in Munich, Germany, drawing millions of visitors.
https://en.wikipedia.org/wiki/Oktoberfest

Nawruz Festival (Persia)
(First celebrated c. 3000 BCE): The Persian New Year, celebrated at the spring equinox, promoting peace and harmony.
https://en.wikipedia.org/wiki/Nowruz

Olympic Games (Modern)
(First held in 1896, Athens): The revival of the ancient Olympic Games, promoting international athletic competition.
https://en.wikipedia.org/wiki/1896_Summer_Olympics

Olympic Games 1912 (Stockholm)
(First held in 1912): The Stockholm Olympics were the first to introduce electronic timing for events.
https://en.wikipedia.org/wiki/1912_Summer_Olympics

Olympic Games 1952 (Helsinki)
(First held in 1952): Marked by the participation of the Soviet Union, highlighting Cold War tensions.
https://en.wikipedia.org/wiki/1952_Summer_Olympics

Olmo Trophy (Venice)
(First held in 1982): A Gallorini family-organized event featuring sports and cultural activities in Olmo di Martellago, Venice (Italy)
(No official link)

Opet Festival (Egypt)
(First celebrated c. 1400 BCE): An ancient Egyptian festival

in Thebes celebrating the connection between the gods Amun, Mut, and the Pharaoh.
https://en.wikipedia.org/wiki/Opet_Festival

Royal Society (London)
(Founded in 1660): One of the oldest scientific institutions in the world, promoting scientific excellence and knowledge sharing.
https://en.wikipedia.org/wiki/Royal_Society

Salone del Mobile (Milan)
(First held in 1961): The world's most prestigious furniture fair, showcasing cutting-edge designs and innovations.
www.salonemilano.com

Tomorrowland
(First held in 2005): One of the largest electronic music festivals in the world, held annually in Belgium.
https://www.tomorrowland.com/

Woodstock (USA)
(First held in 1969): A landmark music festival symbolizing the 1960s counterculture, peace, and love movement.
https://en.wikipedia.org/wiki/Woodstock

World Expos
(First held in 1851): International exhibitions showcasing achievements in technology, culture, and industrial advancements.
https://en.wikipedia.org/wiki/World%27s_fair

Yalta Conference
(Held in 1945): A major political event during World War II where Allied leaders met to discuss the post-war reorganization of Europe.
https://en.wikipedia.org/wiki/Yalta_Conference